The Quiet Man
The Pat Stanton Story

'The Quiet Man'

* * *

The Pat Stanton Story

* * *

As told to
SIMON PIA

SPORTSPRINT PUBLISHING

EDINBURGH

ISBN 0 85976 288 2

Our thanks to the Edinburgh *Evening News*
for permission to reproduce illustrations
on pages 3, 54, 62, 73, 81 and 103.
The remainder are from Pat Stanton's own collection.

Phototypeset by Beecee Typesetting Services
Printed in Great Britain by Bell & Bain Ltd., Glasgow

Contents

CHAPTER ONE

Last Exit from Easter Road

DESPITE the sour taste I was left with when I made my last exit from Easter Road, it has not affected my feelings for Hibs. I grew up in a Hibs family and these things just do not change. Also I reckon I am as keen a Hibs supporter as anybody else, but I cannot say the way I left both as a player and a manager did not have an effect on me.

I was bitterly disappointed both times. I had given all I had for the club yet felt I had been let down on each occasion. One thing it did do was teach me a few lessons about life. I paid the price of loyalty both times and when I returned to be Hibs manager I let my heart rule my head. I knew deep down it was probably a mistake, but I felt I had to do it and owed it to the fans. I could not let them down as they had been so good to me throughout my career and still are today.

But I knew Hibs fans wanted the good times to return when we were renowned for our cavalier and attacking football. Hibs may not have ever heaped up the trophies. No one ever has in Scotland apart from the Old Firm, but the club had something special about it. Hibs had flair and class and everyone knew it. More than all my personal disappointments that was what hurt me the most.

There was no will to achieve this at board level and the place where I felt I would get the greatest encouragement I actually got the least. I got far more at Aberdeen, Dunfermline and Cowdenbeath. The Hibs board during my management just wanted to tick along and get by on what we had. However, I could see we had to spend to get out of the rut the club had fallen into, but money was never forthcoming. I don't know if there ever was or wasn't money available, but one thing I know for sure is I never saw any of it.

There has been a lot of speculation among Hibs fans about my relationship with Kenny Waugh, the chairman at that time. I do not bear a personal grudge against him. That is not my style. I bump into him occasionally and we are civil to each other, but I do believe his board never gave me the backing I needed and never intended to.

My first exit from Easter Road could not have been more different from my last. It was when I moved to Celtic after over fifteen years with Hibs. For a year I had been going through a bad time at the club and had fallen out with Eddie Turnbull. I felt he was making me a scapegoat for other problems at the club. It was also no secret that there were other players at the club who had as much to say as me, but I was the player who said it. I was considered the quiet man but I would still not do certain things Eddie Turnbull demanded and would tell him what I thought. Meanwhile others toed the party line. I had no divine right to keep on playing for Hibs and Turnbull wanted rid of me. However, I was always thankful to Jock Stein for coming in for me and what I went on to achieve proved to many people I was not finished as a player. When I actually left Hibs the only person who shook my hand and wished me well was Tom McNiven. I then walked out the ground alone with a pair of boots under my arm.

When I resigned as Hibs manager it turned into a media circus with television cameras and press hovering around. However, one comment made at the time has bothered me ever since. Jim Kean of the *Daily Record* quoted Kenny Waugh as saying there had been a breakdown in communication between the players and me. It made me livid. The *Record* had just accepted what Kenny Waugh said and had not given me a chance to reply. I do not know if they had tried to contact me for my side of the story, but anyway there was my career in management summed up in one sentence in black and white. Nothing could have been further from the truth and I thought it was irresponsible reporting. Also what really rankled was the comment hardly came from an expert on the game. If there was any breakdown in communication it was between Kenny Waugh and me.

Overall my spell as manager had begun to wear me down. It was a hand-to-mouth existence and there was a limit to what I could do in the circumstances. Every Saturday had become a matter of life and death. A lot of the players at the club were the ones who had got Hibs relegated a few seasons earlier, but I got no encouragement to follow up on players I suggested buying. Maybe the board didn't think I was doing a good enough job with what we had, but I think anybody would have been toiling. However, we did bring through good young players at that time such as Gordon Hunter, Michael Weir, Paul Kane, John Collins, Callum Milne and Brian Rice.

Last exit from Easter Road. My resignation aroused its share of media interest.

They have gone on to prove their value to the club which I think shows we were on the right track. Since then it has also been a bit of a disappointment that, along with my assistants Jimmy O'Rourke and George Stewart, nobody has asked us to scout for players. Some of the people you see scouting for clubs couldn't tell a player if he came up and kicked them in the backside.

Looking back I find it sad that the club which meant so much to me behaved in the way it did. I was also able to contrast it with other clubs when I was a player at Celtic and in management at Aberdeen, Dunfermline and Cowdenbeath. At Celtic I was lucky to have Jock Stein as my manager. Any professional would have loved to play for him. Also both the Fife clubs were good to me when I managed them. However, Aberdeen to my mind were how a club should be run. They are very civilised in a hard game, but they have always wanted to win as much as anybody. They are very competitive and are geared to winning, but realise if you want success on the park and to be a really big club, you have to be big in every way. I hope this lesson has been learned at Easter Road and I believe there is room for optimism with the present board.

Some people have said I was too nice a guy to succeed in management, but these people don't really know me. I know what went wrong at Easter Road and felt I could have turned things around if I had got the chance. When I left, money had to be made available or the board were in trouble. It was just a pity it wasn't more forthcoming at an earlier stage. I never shouted my mouth off because it isn't my way, but I had my views and stuck to them. Finally I had had enough and walked out on the board but have never felt I was deserting the club. How could I, when we go back such a long way?

CHAPTER TWO

A Hibs Heritage

THERE was never any doubt that I would be brought up a Hibs supporter. The whole of my family were Hibs supporters and my father came from the Southside of the city which was a Hibs' stronghold. The club had been founded there in St Mary's Street in 1875 and a lot of people from that area moved out to the Craigmillar housing estate where I grew up after the war.

Of course, it is quite well known now that the club's first captain, Michael Whelehan, was a direct relative of mine on my father's side but, if the truth be told, I was never very aware of this until I started playing for Hibs. It was only then that people started really mentioning it to me. But the Hibs connection did not exist only on my father Michael's side. My mother Bridgit had an uncle, Jimmy Hendren, who played for Hibs and was signed from Cowdenbeath back in 1911. So you could say I had a well-balanced upbringing with a Hibernian heritage on both sides.

My father was very keen on Hibs and naturally, like most boys, I went to my first games at Easter Road with him. I especially remember when Hibs were the first British team to play in the European Cup in 1955. It was also my father who took me to Hampden for the first time and that was to see Hibs lose 1-0 in the Cup Final to Clyde in 1958.

First and foremost, though, my family were just football people. My father had a good knowledge of the game and I have always listened to what he has had to say. Throughout my playing days, even as a schoolboy, he watched me and always gave me good advice. Needless to say, when I was younger I was a bit slow to appreciate it at times, but as I got more mature I could invariably see he had been right. You could also say I was brought up to appreciate good football. Hibs fans in those days were spoiled. My father told me all about the Famous Five and the

The Holy Cross team that won the *Evening News* trophy in 1958. I was not the only one who went on to play as a professional. Back row third from the left is Jimmy McManus who went on to play with Dundee United and Falkirk. Back row second right is Malcolm McPherson who played for Raith Rovers. And in the front on the left you can't fail to spot the shine on Jimmy O'Rourke's toe caps, and that's me and Davy Hogg, who also joined Hibs, with the Shield resting on our kneecaps.

great Gordon Smith. Although Hibs were fading a bit, as I began to appreciate football more, we got another treat with the arrival of Joe Baker on the Scottish football scene.

Meanwhile I was growing up in Craigmillar and I stayed there until I got married in 1968. In my day it wasn't so much a rough area as a tough one. You had to learn to look after yourself at an early age. Then there was plenty of employment, so it didn't have the problems that it has today. I liked the area and the people there and am sorry to see the unemployment and drug problems it has now. But I like to point out to people that Craigmillar folk don't just take it lying down, and they have the Craigmillar Festival Society which is run by local people and does a lot for the community.

I was lucky as I had a typically happy childhood, coming from a solid working-class family. My father worked as a cellar man at the nearby Dryboroughs brewery and my mother worked in a laundry. I have five brothers, three older and two younger. Football took up all our time as

With the ball at my feet and my United Crossroads teammates outside Blackfriars Street in 1956.

that was all there was to do, and we played it day and night. There were always football boots and a ball about the house. These were a lot more innocent days and the big event that I remember was when an Elvis film came to The County, the local picture house. Queues stretched round the block, but you could never hear a bloody thing for all the lassies, togged out in their best gear, screaming their heads off. Mind you, by the end of the picture there was hardly anybody left as they had all been flung out. The ushers at The County in those days were more like a bunch of bouncers.

In those days nearly everyone in Craigmillar supported Hibs or Hearts. The Celtic and Rangers buses leaving from the area only came much later on in the '60s. Also the sectarian aspects of football never cropped up as nobody ever bothered about it. I can honestly say that in all my time at Easter Road never once was religion mentioned. I remember once when I was manager at Easter Road and we were showing some schoolkids round the ground, one of them asked, 'How many of your team are Catholics?' The question took me by surprise. I told her, 'I don't know, dear, I've never thought to ask them.' It was obviously something she wanted to know, but it had never occurred to me. The only thing people were bothered about at Easter Road was whether you were a good player or not. Likewise, there was no antagonism between Hibs and Hearts fans when I was growing up in

Craigmillar. I think it is ridiculous that it has crept in over the years, but I have always got on well with Hearts fans and still do.

But as I said, football was our life. I went to St Francis, the local primary school, and I remember getting picked for my first game. I was so excited that my mother got my brother, who worked in the GPO at that time, to stop off and get me a special pair of black and white hooped socks from Mackenzies sports shop near the old Empire on South Bridge. To go with them, I had the classic old Thompson brown-toed boots. I thought I was Jack the Lad in them, but you only need to take a walk across any park these days to see how things have changed with the expensive equipment the kids have now.

However, as a boy I didn't stand out immediately and never thought then I would go places in the game. I played for St Francis in the Craigmillar Community Cup, a local tournament where the winners played a select drawn from all the other teams. The first year I was selected as a left winger, but the next I played at left half. My father pointed out I was better there and it began to dawn on me it was my truer position.

Around that time I also got picked as inside left for the 'possibles' in the Edinburgh primary schools trials at Warriston. A tall, fair outside left for the 'probables' that day was outstanding. It was Alan Gordon, who was to become a good friend and team mate in later years at Easter Road. Alan played for Murrayburn and was an exceptional schoolboy player.

At that time I took the eleven plus qualifying exam and went on to Holy Cross secondary school. I've always felt it's wrong to pigeon-hole people at such an age, sticking a label on them. In football too many judgements of players are made when they're still under 16. The system benefited the kid who studied, but the harum-scarum brigade would often fall by the wayside. It doesn't mean to say they're less intelligent or less able, but the school system in my day suited more those who didn't make waves.

Anyway, I went to Holy Cross, but must say I didn't really like it. For the first time in my life I encountered watered down snobbery. Here I was: a raw, young lad from Craigmillar travelling across the city to Holy Cross every day, a school with a rugby reputation.

I never felt a part of things at Holy Cross and if you were into football and not academically minded you were looked upon as a young upstart. The difference between the football and rugby groups at the school was brought home to me when our football team went on to win the *Evening News* Shield which was then a prestigious Edinburgh trophy. It had

That's me with the cup and my other Boys Club team United Crossroads. On my right were two of my pals from Craigmillar, the Taylor Twins, Jimmy and Billy. Jimmy McManus is on my left and Roger Anderson, brother of Alan, the Hearts player, is behind me.

never been won by Holy Cross before, but we got little recognition for it and not even a medal. If it had been the rugby team, that would have been another matter. The first XV used to swan about the corridors with colours stitched on their blazers, whereas in contrast in the shield-winning team photograph I had a hole in my jersey.

Still I didn't really rate myself a special player. Although I was picked for the Leith schools team, I never made it into the all-Edinburgh select. However, I began to get an inkling I might be going somewhere in this game when I was chosen for the school's first team when I was still only in second year. Holy Cross were to play Bellevue who were rated as a top school team at the time, and another young lad was promoted that day who was even younger than me. It was Jimmy O'Rourke.

The teacher who encouraged us was Jock Coleman, himself a Holy Cross legend. He was the driving force behind football at the school and one of the few who had time for the 'toerags' who played football. However, Jock had his own unique style and was never one for buttering you up. If you scored a hat trick in the World Cup Final, Jock would say, 'You had no a bad game, son.' Even when I went on to play with Hibs, Jimmy and I would bump into Jock who would ask how we were doing and we always felt Jock thought we were doing 'no bad'.

I always thought it was a pity that Holy Cross had this attitude as the school produced a lot of good footballers. Around my time lads like

The Salvesen Boys club side that won the Under 17 Scottish Cup in 1961.

Davy Hogg joined Hibs and George Brough, Terry Christie and Pat Hughes went on to do quite well in the professional game. But anyone from that time will tell you the star of them all was Jimmy. Straight away he stood out as something special. You knew then he was going to make it. Although I was older than Jimmy, we got to know each other and went on to become great mates. After one summer holiday I remember my boys' club team United Crossroads taking on Jimmy's team Rosehall Thistle. Jimmy had filled out over the holidays into that distinctive frame he still has today and took us on virtually single-handed and beat us. Jock Coleman used to say he only ever bothered to tell Jimmy about a Saturday fixture as it didn't really matter how many of the others turned up as long as O'Rourke was there. Jimmy went on to play for Scotland schoolboys and it was no surprise when he turned out for Hibs against Utrecht in the Fairs Cup in 1962 when he was still only 16.

Although I may sound disgruntled about my old school, I don't think they can complain about Jimmy and me as it was their two former pupils who scored the goals that won Hibs the League Cup in 1972, the club's first major trophy since the early '50s. Looking back now on my schooldays, I realise I should have applied myself a lot more. I liked history and geography, subjects you needed some imagination for, and was quite good at art. However, Latin was something I could never

That's me behind the East of Scotland Cup Bonnyrigg had just won after beating Tranent 4-3.

fathom and I still don't see the point of it. Today I still read a lot, but I was lucky that football just fell into place in my life. It seemed like a natural progression and I went on to join Hibs straight from school.

While I was at school I started playing for boys' clubs, first St Mary's the cathedral's team, and then with United Crossroads and Salvesen Boys' club. United Crossroads were run by Eric Gardner who was well known throughout Edinburgh. Eric was a fitness fanatic who made sure he instilled the right values in boys at the club in Blackfriars Street. If he meets you today he still talks to you as if you were a kid. John Greig and Sandy Jardine were at Crossroads at that time as well as Ken Buchanan, who was as good with his feet as his fists in those days.

Eric Gardner's main thing was that the lads enjoyed themselves and taking part was as important, if not more so, than winning. Likewise when I moved on to Salvesen, Bob Moncur was from the same mould as Eric. With Salvesen under-17s we won the Scottish Cup, beating Port Glasgow 3-2. It was also around this time that other clubs began to show an interest in me such as Dundee and Chelsea. By now I was developing into a real footballer and I can see I learned a lot from these men and my father. They had lived for a few years and knew a bit more about life than me. We were taught the one thing that football will

guarantee you is disappointment, but it is how you react to the
disappointment that is important. You can be having a good run then
get beaten. The most important thing now is the next game and if you
bounce back or not.

These men also taught what I feel are good values. Recently I watched
a game in Harrison Park where the laddies were booting the ball out of
the park with ten minutes to go so they could hang on to a one-goal
lead. Never once as a juvenile was I ever told to do that. If I had done it I
am sure I would have been in trouble. Similarly football is far too
competitive at too early an age in Scotland. You see adults in the parks
screaming at kids to win at all costs. This attitude leaves its imprint and
works its way right up to the top. The minute enjoyment takes second
place to winning for youngsters, something has gone wrong. Also you
go into some houses nowadays and there is a cabinet brimming with
medals. Then you find out they belong to a laddie who is only 15.
Surely something is out of proportion. In my time we got hardly any
medals at such a young age and the few you got you really treasured.

Another problem for the game is how boys are marked out to make it
by the time they're 14. Too often, though, the late developer gets left
behind. With competition so important, the survival of the fittest takes
precedence over talent. It can be a great disappointment for boys if they
feel they're discarded too young. Encouragement and enjoyment are the
two main things they should be brought up on. There will be plenty of
competition and coaching ahead of them, but get them to master the
basic skills first.

I was first invited along to Easter Road to train with Hibs when I was
14 by Jimmy McClory, a friend of a relative of mine. I used to train
Tuesday and Thursday nights, but most of that was lapping the park.
You were lucky if you ever got on the pitch and that was only in the
close season. But it was great to be around the club and use the same
dressing room as my then hero, Joe Baker. Another player I really
admired was Alex Young of Hearts. It didn't matter that he played for
Hearts, it was just he was such a good player. I think it's a great pity fans
don't mix in the same way as they did then, going to each other's games
and even standing together on the terraces at derby games.

On a wider scale my heroes were people like Di Stefano and, of
course, Pele whom I well remember watching in the 1958 World Cup.
Another player from 1958 I particularly remember is Nils Liedholm of
Sweden who now manages Roma. He scored a penalty with his right
foot, but the referee made him retake it. So what does Liedholm do? He
sticks it in with his left this time. Now that was what I call a player.

So by now I was 16 and about to leave school. As I said, other clubs were beginning to take an interest in me, but deep down I was hoping Hibs would come right out and sign me. However, it was not to be quite as simple as that.

CHAPTER THREE

The Green Rookie

ALTHOUGH all I ever wanted to do was play for Hibs, I almost never signed for them and could well have ended up playing at Dunfermline under Jock Stein. I was coming up to leave school in 1961 and was under the impression Hibs had registered me as a player. In those days clubs had public trials where signed players took on a select of other promising players the club was interested in. Since I had been with Hibs from the age of 14 I assumed the forms I had filled in had been sent on to the SFA. Before the game the strips were being handed out in the dressing room and I was passed by. I asked what was happening and was taken aback when I was told I was not a signed player. So I ended up in the away team dressing room. Immediately I told my father about it and we went to see Walter Galbraith, Hibs' manager.

To say the least we were a bit niggled. Why had they not signed me? If they didn't want me, they could have let me know. Instead they had left me under the impression they had registered me as one of their players while the forms were stuck in a drawer somewhere at Easter Road. We were not given a satisfactory explanation straight away. It was then that I first made contact with Jock Stein. Little did I know then how our paths were going to cross throughout my career.

At that time he was beginning to make a name for himself as a manager with Dunfermline and he asked me over for a trial. I was flattered by his interest and played right half against St Mirren. I was up against Tommy Gemmill who was in the Saints team that had won the Scottish Cup along with others that night such as Gerry Baker, Leishman and Bryceland. I thought I got a real chasing off Gemmill that night, but obviously Stein saw something he liked as he wanted me to sign.

Alex Cameron points out they're pulling up the gang plank as we board a trawler on a trip to Grimsby. Tam McNiven is on the left and manager Walter Galbraith, every bit the matinee idol, stands between me and Jimmy O'Rourke. That's a member of the press gang in the background.

The next thing I knew a Hibs scout appeared at my door, prompted no doubt by Stein's interest in me. My father was really angry. I could tell he wanted me to play for Hibs, but he felt they were mucking me around. He went back in to see Walter Galbraith, told him I was Hibs minded and they'd better make their mind up if they wanted me. Hibs finally acted and registered me as a Hibs player. I thought Hibs had not behaved very well. I don't know if it was just plain carelessness or not but they should have made my position clear to me one way or the other. This had dragged on for a four-month period and other boys had been getting signed. They always said they wanted me, but were doing nothing about it. But I suppose they could have had other things on their minds as it was the season Hibs almost got relegated.

Meanwhile they farmed me out to junior side Bonnyrigg Rose which was to prove a great education. I enjoyed myself there and soon learned what it was all about, moving up from juveniles to juniors. Many junior players were former professionals who had been reinstated, so you soon learned football wasn't just a stroll in the park.

I get in a header against Morton in the League Cup semi-final at Ibrox in 1963. This was my second game for Hibs, but we lost.

Bill Durie, Bonnyrigg's trainer, was a smashing guy and the committee were a good bunch. The only thing one of them could ever say was 'D'ye ken, son, Sean Connery used to play for us?' True enough, but there was more to the club than that. They were the best team in the east and we beat Tranent 4-3 that year in the East of Scotland Cup at Easter Road. Willie Paul our goalkeeper went on to play for Third Lanark and eventually became a famous bowls player. The left winger Billy Neil went to Milwall and Bobby Duncan had played centre forward with Bonnyrigg shortly before me.

I had been playing right half at juvenile, but Bonnyrigg pushed me forward to inside right. I was the only professional in the team and quite a lot was expected of you, but as long as you kept your end up there were no problems. It was at Bonnyrigg that I learned to tackle and realised how I had been ignoring a key piece of advice my father had been trying to drum into me. As a juvenile I was a bit fine on the ball and didn't get stuck in. I didn't feel it was necessary to have a good tackle. So junior football was a rude awakening. You either stood up to a player on the park if you wanted to go anywhere, or you were trampled on. After a few games I soon changed my attitude and I like to think my tackling developed into as good a part of my game as any

Keepie uppie for the camera in 1964.

Scoring from four yards against Raith Rovers in the mid-60s. As you can see, we got not bad crowds for such a fixture in those days.

other aspect. It taught me the lesson at times you have to get back to the basics and throw niceties out of the window.

It was also at Bonnyrigg that I came across tactics for the first time, but we ended up on the receiving end of them. We were going to play Easthouse Lily and expected to roll over them. Their captain was a Craigmillar lad Johnny Mochan, a dapper little guy and great football enthusiast. He was playing at the back, pulling all the strings, and they won 4-1. We were humbled by this defeat, and going home on the bus was the first time I tried to understand how they had done it. They played a fluid system coming up the park as one, defenders included, and retreated as a unit. When Jock Stein came to Hibs, he was the first person I had come across who would warn you how another team would play, and needless to say he was never wrong.

Although I played inside right with Bonnyrigg, my father told me my best position was at the back. I knew this myself, but because I could play in the middle of the park and score, it was maybe inevitable that managers would want to play me there throughout most of my career. By this time I was super fit as I would train with Hibs during the week

Football can be a tiring game. Here I look as if I'm about to drop off during a game.

and spend two nights with Bonnyrigg. I have always enjoyed training and never found it a chore. It is vital that players develop good habits in this area as early as possible. If you don't you will only suffer later. Also, develop good habits on the training pitch and you will take them and the correct attitude into a game.

We played the old W formation with one wing half more attack-minded while the other would be more defensive. We were virtually playing 4-2-4 although we didn't know it at the time. A lot of teams had started playing it against Hibs without even knowing it. Gordon Smith used to torment full backs so the centre half would inevitably get drawn out as Smith went past his man. So they had to have an extra man back covering. Suddenly the press latched on to 4-2-4 but I saw it more as a natural progression rather than some amazing new development.

By the time I left Bonnyrigg I had passed by many of the lads my age who had stayed on at Easter Road. I was getting a regular game every Saturday whereas not all of them were, and junior football had also toughened me up. I had also matured in other ways. I had thrown off the childishness whereby I did not like my father watching me. He was now watching me regularly at Easter Road. My time at Bonnyrigg paid off because I only spent six weeks in the reserves before I made my first-team debut.

Hibs were going through a transition period. Joe Baker had left two seasons before and they had narrowly escaped relegation at the end of the 1962-63 season. I started the new season full-time with Hibs along with a couple of other newcomers. Hibs had signed Tom McNiven from Third Lanark as trainer and Neil Martin from Queen of the South who was an instant success. I wasn't nervous about going full-time as I had been training there for a long time and people like Jimmy O'Rourke were there on the ground staff. Mature players at the club such as Tommy Preston, Tam Leishman and Willie Toner were on hand to give us youngsters a lot of good advice. After one game where I played well, Willie Toner pointed out to me that I shouldn't expect the next game to be the same. Never go into a game with preconceived notions, he said. Sometimes you could be too complacent or treat the opposition with too much respect. He also pointed out to me the truth about the corny cliché that football is a game of two halves. The half-time break does make the second half another game. So either way you have got a chance to improve, or then again you'd better be careful you don't rest on your first-half performance.

I found Walter Galbraith a decent man and held no grudge despite the carry-on over registering me. He never set the heather on fire at Easter Road, but he knew a good player when he saw one. Walter signed Willie Hamilton whose career was under a shadow at Tynecastle, and Pat Quinn from Motherwell. Both were excellent midfield players, but

Hibs' five-a-side team at Olive Bank, Musselburgh. (Left to right) Eric Stevenson, Peter Cormack, me, John Grant and our keeper Tommy Preston. July 1963.

Willie was a different class. Also John Parke, a fine left back, joined the club from Linfield. Walter also introduced youngsters Bobby Duncan, Billy Simpson and another Holy Cross boy Davy Hogg and myself. Although Walter Galbraith moved on within a year, he had brought together players that Jock Stein, I am sure, would have turned into a great team if he had stayed longer with Hibs. Then in October 1963 I made my first-team debut against Motherwell at inside right. One of their defenders adopted the old approach to any novice. He tried to kick me right round the park, but I wasn't intimidated as I had been kicked by far harder men at Bonnyrigg. Also I could see him coming a mile away. I scored one that day, but we lost 4-3. My goal was a left-footer where I turned on the edge of the box. I was surprised the keeper didn't save it, but I did know what I was trying to do with it. I think my father was more excited about my debut than I was and I felt I took it in my stride.

My next game was the League Cup semi-final against Morton at Ibrox, but we could only draw 1-1 and lost the replay. A young lad called Stanton missed an absolute sitter that could have taken Hibs into the final. Soon after I played Dundee who were some team then with Gilzean, Cousins and Penman playing. However, I was also up against a legend that day. Gordon Smith was virtually at the end of his career but

I've never been one for strips with patterns or a fancy sheen on them. This to my mind was one of the best Hibs strips you get, circa 1964. (Left to right) John Fraser, Tam Leishman, Willie Wilson, Myself, John McNamee, Jimmy Stevenson.
Front (Left to right) Jimmy O'Rourke, Willie Hamilton, Stan Vincent, Neil Martin, Jim Scott.

I still remember that day he left me standing every time I went near him, even when I tried to kick him.

By now I was moved back to left half where I felt happier. I was also lucky as players competing for the half-back positions at Easter Road were getting on a bit, so here was a chance for me to break through. Often good young players can miss out because such a good well-established player holds a position for so long. Just think about any young right wingers trying to make it at Easter Road in Gordon Smith's day. They had no chance. As in other things in life, football is often about being in the right place at the right time.

I also had a feeling something was going to happen at Easter Road. Hibs were still in the shadow of the Famous Five and there had been a dramatic drop in standards. When I first started training at Easter Road, Bobby Johnstone was still there. Eddie Turnbull and Willie Ormond had played in the 1958 Cup Final alongside Joe Baker. In 1961 Hibs had reached the semi finals of the Fairs Cup only to lose out to Roma after a third match play off in Rome. Yet they had almost got relegated two seasons later. Heads were beginning to get buried even deeper in the sand, but a new manager was to change that. I felt I had been learning a lot in the game, but playing under Jock Stein was to be a real eye opener. I only wish the experience had lasted longer as we all felt we were on the verge of something.

CHAPTER FOUR

The Big Man and the Will o' the Wisp

NEAR the end of the 1963/64 season Walter Galbraith resigned and we were training on the pitch at Easter Road when we saw Willie Harrower, the chairman, come down the tunnel with Jock Stein. This was to be our first meeting with the new manager and it was fitting that it should be on the pitch as Stein was the embodiment of the new 'track suit' manager. Walter Galbraith had been from the old school, always wearing a suit and never taking training, whereas here was Jock Stein, only a few minutes in the job, and he was out sizing up his new charges.

Even then people knew Jock Stein had charisma. He had authority and commanded respect as though it was the most natural thing in the world. However, he had that perfect balance where he was not too aloof or distant from the players and they felt he understood them. He also had great common sense and judgment. He knew exactly the right time and the right way to explain something to somebody so it would have exactly the right effect.

I had an advantage as I already knew Jock from my trial at Dunfermline, so he came over and asked how I was doing and had a chat. From that day on I was to have an excellent relationship with him and I always felt I could speak freely with him. A lot of people were in awe of him and often players would be too scared to say something to him. If you weren't playing well at half time you would make sure you didn't catch his eye in the dressing room. But I always felt I could say anything to him within reason.

Years later when I was sent off against Red Star Belgrade in Australia on tour with Celtic, Stein strode into the dressing room after the game. In front of everybody he said 'What the hell's a player with your experience doing something stupid like that for?' The Yugoslav had hit

Jock Stein's full squad at Easter Road in 1964.

me in the face so I'd hit him back. I was still smarting a bit and snapped back. 'What would you have done in my place?' The other players were taken aback at this, waiting for Stein's reaction. But the big man just shook his head and broke out in a huge grin.

He immediately made an impact with the players and soon the place was buzzing. His training methods were completely new and, as I said, he was the first manager to come to training. Tom McNiven was a great trainer with fresh ideas and he and Stein worked very well together. Tom introduced stretching exercises. That may not seem much nowadays, but at that time it was something I had never done before. Stein also had the great knack of making training interesting. He would vary it and we started to use the pitch and practise with the ball a lot earlier in the week. Till then hard slog had come first and any work on technique or skill was almost an afterthought left to later on in the week.

Another thing about Jock Stein was he had an uncanny knack of almost immediately being able to tell what a player's best position was. He had played me at right half in my trial at Dunfermline and moved me to the back as soon as he came to Easter Road. There I teamed up with big John McNamee whom Stein signed from Celtic.

With Walter Galbraith I had started at inside right, then played as a half back, operating in midfield. I even played on the left wing in one game at Love Street. Although I got two goals that day, we had got something wrong. Normally you get the full back kicking the winger, but that day it was the other way round with me kicking lumps out of him and chasing him up and down the touchline. But I could always play on the left though I'm naturally right-footed. I practised with my left to make sure I was adequate with two feet. A lot of chances are missed by forwards because of their lack of two good feet, and defenders regularly miscontrol because the ball arrives at their wrong foot. No matter what anybody says, hard practice can develop either foot. It is only the exceptions that can maybe get away without it, such as Puskas. His right leg could have been wooden, his left was that good.

Anyway Stein encouraged us to work on all these wee aspects of our game and soon it was paying dividends. The Summer Cup was introduced for that close season and we got in courtesy of Hearts being on tour in America. We beat Dunfermline and then Kilmarnock in the semis. The final was delayed till August due to the typhoid epidemic in Aberdeen. After two legs we were still level and Aberdeen won the toss to stage the third match. Willie Hamilton blasted us into an early lead before Ernie Winchester equalised. Then we got a penalty. During training at old Meadowbank, Stein had nominated me as penalty taker. It was unusual to give the responsibility to a young player, but obviously he had faith in me. Unfortunately I missed it, but Jim Scott and Peter Cormack scored to give us a comfortable victory. After that I rarely took penalties. I remember one against East Fife at Bayview and another in my only hat-trick for Hibs in a game against Clyde. But of course my most famous penalty is the one I took in the shoot-out against Leeds in the UEFA Cup. That game was unusual as everyone scored except for me. Billy Bremner crashed his against the bar, but it went in. That game should never have gone to penalties as we were well on top of Leeds and had what I still feel today was a perfectly good goal by Alan Gordon disallowed.

With one trophy behind us, Stein once again displayed his panache as a manager. As Hearts were in the Fairs Cup that season Stein thought he would give Hibs fans a taste of Europe as well. Jock Stein was a big thinker so it was only natural that he should bring the best to Easter

Pat Delaney, son of the great Jimmy Delaney of Celtic, gets in to put one past Billy Simpson and Willie Wilson. 1965.

Road. Real Madrid came in October and it turned out a great night for Hibs.

Another aspect of Stein's talent as a manager was his sense of publicity and how he handled the media. Here he had projected Hibs onto centre stage with the media clambering all over Easter Road, while Hearts' European tie was small fry in comparison. On the Saturday before the Real game we had beaten Kilmarnock 2-1 and John Rafferty of *The Scotsman* had predicted we would be hammered 7-0. That night as we were celebrating in the bath after our 2-0 victory, Stein brought John into the dressing room and announced to us, 'Here's the guy who said you would lose 7-0.' Then he turned on him and asked how he could have written that when the game had not been played. Of course it was all good-natured, but underneath Stein was making his point — never dare write off any team of mine. It was also good psychology with the players. He was telling us not to listen to what the media says. They will always back the big clubs. What you know about yourself is more important than how anyone else builds you up or puts you down.

Before that game Stein warned us how Real Madrid would play. Their build-up would start on the halfway line and they would come at us in groups. So as soon as their right back would start moving to the halfway line to start a move, our front four would move over to close that part of the pitch down. Likewise, when they tried it on the left we would move men over there. That was the first time anybody had briefed me before a game and of course Stein was spot-on as usual. Your respect for the man could only grow as he obviously had such a thorough knowledge of the game. Without a doubt he was streets ahead of anyone else in Scotland.

It turned out a great night and we wore green shorts at Real Madrid's request so they would look their best in their famous all-white strip. That game was also memorable for me because here I was just turned 20 and pitched directly up against Ferenc Puskas. Puskas, along with his team mate Di Stefano and Pele, was one of the greatest players in the world. Only a couple of years earlier he had mesmerised Hampden in that magnificent final against Eintracht Frankfurt. However, I was in for a rude awakening. Early in the second half Puskas went over the ball at me and caught me on the right ankle. Maybe I was doing too good a job on him and should have taken it as a back-handed compliment, but it disappointed me. I thought Puskas might have been above that as I wasn't kicking him and it was strictly a friendly. Then again, it demonstrates that football is a hard game, and to stay at the top even the most skilful of players have to have that hard streak in them.

That night we silenced our critics and treated the 30,000 fans to a great display. Peter Cormack scored our first and in the second half Real's defender Zoco deflected in a Pat Quinn free kick. But the most striking thing that night was the brilliant form of Willie Hamilton. This was his stage and the fact he was playing against Puskas and Real Madrid that night spurred Willie on.

I will always remember with two minutes to go Real got a corner and Amancio went to take it. We were all back in the box when eventually up strolls Willie. He walked over to me and the crowd obviously thought here's the old head coming to give the young boy a bit of advice, settle any nerves and tell him who to mark. Instead Willie says 'Here, Pat son, they tell me you get a watch for playing this lot.' He was right too. I still have mine and it keeps good time, but that remark was typical of the man. Nothing phased him. He could have been running a park game that night, never mind playing Real Madrid.

I still look on that game as Willie's night and must say he was the most talented player I every played with or against. Many people are often surprised when I say this, but I even rated him above Jim Baxter whom I played against. One time when I was at Celtic, Roy Aitken and Tommy Burns, just young lads at the time, asked me whom I rated as the best

I look on with John Fraser as Peter Cormack drives off Stan Vincent's head. I think they stuck a tee in it, but Stan wouldn't have noticed the difference. We got a row for this bit of promotion from Jock Stein as he didn't like us doing anything at all on a Friday. February 1965.

player I had seen. As I told them about Willie they seemed a bit surprised. Just then big Stein came dripping out the showers. He had overheard what I was saying and had come out to lend his authority to my view that Willie was one of the best ever.

The tragedy about Willie was he was wayward. When Jock Stein was there he could keep Willie under control. Not long after Stein had arrived he gave Willie a dressing down in front of everyone in the dressing room. He called him a disgrace for wasting his great ability on drink and sent him away for a few weeks. It seemed to do the trick. Willie came back and behaved with Stein. Maybe it was because he believed that here was a man with greater talent as a manager than Willie had as a player. The way he could handle all sorts of players was part of Stein's magic and he went on to do it with another great player, Jimmy Johnstone. If Willie had had Stein's guidance throughout his career, things could have been very different for him.

Willie would come in after the game and throw his boots against the wall. 'You're all a bunch of cowboys and I'm the only decent player here,' he would say. Nobody would say anything as we all thought, 'If you're comparing us with you, Willie, you're probably right.'

He was also not the best of trainers and only ever wanted to work with the ball, skipping out on the basics. But he had a great answer for his critics: 'Do you ever see a golfer running around a golf course?' There are many stories about Willie, with some good ones in Stewart Brown's book *Hibernian Greats*. There are also a few you couldn't repeat in a book for all the family. He was a one-off who didn't abide by the rules. He turned up once for a Scotland trip to Italy with only a toothbrush in his top pocket and his boots. He also went on an American tour with only a wee grip for his luggage. When he was presented with a silver platter in Ottawa he had nowhere to put it so he bent it in two and squeezed it into his bag.

Willie was a terrific guy and was good with young players. He could always give you a few good tips, but that was only if you could get him to sit still long enough. He also had that nasty streak which good players need to stop themselves getting roughed up. As I said referring to Puskas, the great players can hand it out as much as anybody.

After the Real game our great run continued. We went to Ibrox and there was a famous showdown in the tunnel between Willie and Jim Baxter before the game. It was all in good fun, but each of them was telling the other what he was going to do with him and how he was going to run the game. Meanwhile the rest of the players just listened in, relishing the prospect that lay ahead. I hold Jim Baxter in the highest esteem and know he is one of the greatest players Scotland has ever produced, but Hamilton proved that day he was master. We won 4-2 despite being behind twice with Willie dictating the play. I reckon he was the only player who could have done that to Jim Baxter.

Willie was superb with both feet and had an incredible long loping stride over that all-important first ten yards. He was also very good in

John Baxter heads clear in our Scottish Cup win against Rangers in 1965.

the air. Willie was a key part of our success that season when I felt we had a great chance of winning both the league and the cup. Also Hibs were reasserting themselves once again as the top team in Edinburgh. In the New Year's game at Tynecastle we won 1-0 thanks to a superb goal from Willie. He had drifted to the bye-line and Jim Cruikshanks, Hearts goalkeeper, wasn't expecting anything. A normal player would surely cut it back for a cross from that impossible angle, but Willie Hamilton was not an ordinary player. Somehow he screwed a beautiful shot into the roof of the net.

We were now competing with Kilmarnock and Hearts for the league and we were about to go on and complete our first league double over Rangers since the 1902/3 season. Over 40,000 packed into Easter Road for our home league game against them, and Neil Martin scored the only goal. Neil was tremendous in the air. A tall wiry lad from Tranent, Hibs had got him for a snip from Queen of the South. He was a similar type of player to Alan Gordon, but maybe a bit more direct.

Things were really rolling by now, but suddenly the Hibs season fell apart. Jock Stein resigned and moved to Celtic, but he did stay on long enough to guide us through our third meeting with Rangers that season in the quarter final of the cup.

An even bigger crowd turned out at Easter Road and it was a fitting farewell for Stein. He obviously loved beating Rangers as he was to prove regularly over the next decade at Parkhead. We were drawing 1-1 with minutes to go when Willie Hamilton ghosted in on a free kick to glance the ball in.

It was indeed a great climax for Jock Stein's career with Hibs, but I was deeply disappointed and angry that Stein was going. I always felt that Celtic could have waited till the end of the season and still don't know who was responsible for the timing of the move. Undoubtedly it had an effect on us. We all knew that Celtic were Stein's first love and if he was going to leave Easter Road it would be to go there. I also believe they are the only club that could have taken him away at that time. Another cruel blow was that his new Celtic team then beat us in the league which ruined our chances of the title. We also lost 2-0 in the semi-finals against Dunfermline who in turn were beaten 3-2 in the final by Celtic. That was to be just the start of his magnificent achievements at Celtic. But little did I know then that I was going to be reunited with Jock Stein at the end of my playing career.

I was to miss Stein as not only did he have a great knowledge of the game, but he was full of good advice on how to conduct yourself. He liked his players to behave themselves and stressed to us how fortunate we were to be in the position we were. There are hundreds, if not thousands, he would tell us, who would love to be in your place, so do not abuse it. He also told us always to go to supporters' functions if we were asked. He was a great man for the people and would emphasise continually that the fans were the lifeblood of the game.

At training he would often stand in the middle of the park as we were lapping it and call players over one by one to have a private chat. It could be about anything, but he would set you right and give you a bit of advice where no one else could. He also would not go on too much about a game after the match. Maybe he would have a go at you, but he left most of it till Monday or Tuesday when you yourself had had time to think about what you had done wrong. Once against Hearts he warned me about Willie Wallace, a player he admired and one I was not at all surprised to see him sign just after he went to Celtic. Wallace liked to come in from the inside left position, stepping with the ball on to his right foot. Stein told me to overlap a yard or so to the right when he was coming at me so I would be right with him. Sure enough, during the game Willie Wallace did just this and as he was cutting into his right I remembered what Stein had told me. But it was too late because just as it clicked, Willie let one fly and it was in the back of the net.

A fine bit of marking. Here is the half back line of John Baxter, John McNamee and myself wandering around in a daze.

Stein was also a wily pragmatist. Once I got booked for booting the ball away after a poor refereeing decision. On Monday morning at training, Stein pulled me up about it. He said, 'See that caution you picked up, it was really stupid. If you'd been booked already that would have been you in for an early bath. I'll show you a better way of expressing your anger. Next time it happens, pick the ball up instead. As long as that ball is in your hands no one is going to be sticking it in the back of the net. The opposition will be waiting for a free kick, so walk towards them with the ball. The ref will notice and think what a nice, sporting gesture. Then drop it just before you hand it over so it rolls away a wee bit. You've wasted a few more seconds and by now everyone in your team should be well positioned. The ref won't give you a row for that and you will have wasted more time than if you had kicked the ball away.' Of course I could see he was right. That was Stein all over. He had so many aspects to him. A great leader full of sound advice, and crafty with it.

Anyway, the inevitable happened and Stein left. Eddie Turnbull was then the favourite to get the job, but it was a bit of a turn up when it went to Bob Shankly who was a great friend of Jock Stein. Bob, though, was very different from the Big Man.

CHAPTER FIVE

European Nights and On the Road with Hibs

BOB SHANKLY had been very successful at Dundee and I always liked him. He was a very honest man and had a good idea of what made a player. We also knew he was into attacking football from the way his Dundee sides had played and he had no time for what he called 'hammer throwers'. He and Stein were great pals, but you couldn't get two more different men. Big Stein would dominate any company he walked into and handled people brilliantly. Bob on the other hand was a quiet, reserved man who was content to stay in the background chainsmoking his endless supplies of fags. However when Bob Shankly said something, you could believe it. I liked that about him.

Considering the circumstances when Bob took over you could not expect much of him in retrieving anything from that season. I think whoever had taken the job would have been toiling. Also, whoever would like to try and step into Jock Stein's shoes? Anyway, he didn't have enough time to do anything in the rest of that season.

He inherited some very good players at Easter Road and a lot of credit was due to Walter Galbraith. In Stein's short spell his main buys were John McNamee and Joe Davis. Big John was the sort of guy you definitely preferred to play with rather than against. Joe Davis was a stylish left back from Third Lanark who developed into a penalty ace. Joe scored 43 goals for Hibs, some record for a full back, but he owed a lot of them to Eric Stevenson. Eric was a very good winger who would regularly cut into the box whereas too many wingers tend to just hug the touchline. Eric got great balls from Pat Quinn who had come from Motherwell. Pat was a clever player who was great at releasing the ball at exactly the right time to bring the winger into play. Wingers need players like Pat as they are often not the brightest of people, but that

35

didn't apply to Eric. Peter Cormack had also begun to make a name and such was his form there was going to be continual transfer controversy surrounding him over the next couple of seasons. Peter would go on to play with Nottingham Forest before joining Bob Shankly's wee brother's team. Bobby Duncan had found his true position thanks to Jock Stein changing him from centre forward into an exciting overlapping right back.

However, we were soon to lose Willie Hamilton to Aston Villa and Neil Martin went to Sunderland. But Bob began to bring in new players and I was to be pushed backwards and forwards from midfield to centre back over the next few years. John Madsen, a good steady Danish centre back, took over from John McNamee when he went to Newcastle and another defender, Alan Cousins, a big scholarly type with a wee shuffle, joined us from Dundee. Allan McGraw arrived from Morton and although he was not very big, he was exceptional in the air. He was also a very brave player and proved it in the League Cup semi-final against Dundee in the 1967/68 season. Allan had gone off injured, but came back on with a heavily bandaged leg. As I saw him coming on I turned to whoever was next to me and said it would be just like him to score the winner and, sure enough, Allan did it sliding in on his backside. Colin Stein was another who made his breakthrough at this time, coming to us from Armadale Thistle. He was a wholehearted player, but I was quite surprised at his £100,000 transfer to Rangers as I thought it was a bit premature. He was to be replaced by a great player, Joe McBride. Joe had the bad luck to get a bad injury in Celtic's European Cup season and he slowed down a bit after that. But he played some great football with Hibs and was one of the best I have ever seen in front of goal. If he was through with just the goalkeeper to beat you could always put your money on Joe, and that is something you cannot say about a lot of strikers who seem to freeze in that position.

Throughout Bob Shankly's spell Hibs played great football and stuck to our cavalier tradition. It was in the post-Ramsey era and defensive football was beginning to take a grip. However, we stuck to our style and some would say we paid for it. We didn't win anything, but came close in the League Cup in the semi final in 1965 and the final in 1968. We also established ourselves as the top Edinburgh team, beating Hearts regularly, and this was to be the trend for the next decade. Also we went on to have some classic tussles with Jock Stein's great Celtic teams. Our form could be very inconsistent over that period, but one of the main reasons for this were the crowds we got. They were not what they should have been at times. That team played some great football, but

With Joe Davis and Willie Hamilton at Niagara Falls in 1967. That's the old Edinburgh coat of arms on Willie's Hibs blazer. You can call me old-fashioned, but I think it was a lot better than the one we have now which would look more at home on a beer bottle.

after a good crowd against Celtic we would be playing against a thousand or so at Arbroath. When I was later to play with Celtic you had atmosphere all the time. You could always react to atmosphere and your concentration was sharper. Imagine Frank Sinatra performing in front of ten people at Portobello Town Hall or to a full house at the Albert Hall. I don't have to tell you where you'd get the better performance.

Occasions, though, when we never had to worry about crowds were our European ties at Easter Road. We had some great ones over this period and it was part of the game I really relished. Although we never won a trophy, we regularly got into Europe through our league position. I was even privileged as a fan, watching European football at Easter Road when Hibs pioneered British entry into the European Cup. That inaugural year we got to the semi-finals only to lose out to Rheims led by the great Raymond Kopa. I also remember watching the infamous encounter with Barcelona at Easter Road and Bobby Kinloch's penalty that started it all. I was training with Hibs at the time and Bobby was taking penalties in the top goal the day before the game and kept

Too many chiefs: here I am in the Rocky Mountains in 1967. I think my pal went on to become President, and that's Jimmy O'Rourke in fancy dress on my left.

missing by miles. When Hibs got the penalty nobody wanted to take it at first. So I turned to my mate on the terracing and said the last person they should give it to was Bobby. But up strode Bobby and did the business and he has always been remembered for it since then. That was when the rammy started, with the fracas on the pitch carrying on down the tunnel after the game. When I was back in at training I remember admiring the nice little job the Barcelona players had made of kicking in the referee's door. Despite these horror stories you hear of taking on foreign teams, I must say I never had any bad experiences.

My first trip abroad was to Cannes in France at the end of the 1964 season and one thing we didn't do was go to the pictures. My first real taste of Europe apart from the Madrid game was also against a Spanish side. In October 1965 we lost out in the third match against Valencia. We had both won 2-0 at home and we tossed for third match advantage in the referee's room. They won both the toss and the game. Our next foray into Europe was in the 1967/68 season when we beat Porto 3-0 at Easter Road. We were lucky to get a quick penalty in the replay as Peter Cormack was sent off and we held on to go through 4-3 on aggregate.

Probably our next tie was Hibs' most famous in Europe and the one

Bobby Duncan and I enjoy ourselves watching the others sweat it out at training. He had just broken his leg against Celtic while I had broken my toe at Airdrie (1968).

that is mentioned to me most regularly. The first leg was in Naples where we lost 4-1 to a hat trick from the Brazilian Cane. Also Altafini was to score against us and it was not to be his last goal against Hibs. He had starred in AC Milan's European Cup team in 1963 and was one of the best I have seen. When he scored in Naples he was still round behind the goals celebrating with the fans when we kicked off again. Napoli were so confident that they didn't even bring Altafini over for the next game, which was a good thing for us if you consider the damage he did when he came on as Juventus' substitute in our 1974 tie. But no Italian team thought they could lose three goals, let alone five.

However, some might want to blame the young trialist they had in goal. His name was Dino Zoff. But that night you could have had both Zoff and Lev Yashin in goal and we would still have scored five. The night before the game their coach Pesaola watched a training session from the directors' box with a large whisky in his hand. He needed another the next night when we were finished with them.

Bobby Duncan scored early on with a superb 40-yard shot into the roof of the net. The manner in which Bobby scored played a big part in our win that night. It happened nice and early and it was so spectacular it really got the crowd roaring right behind us. It also made them think: if this is what their defenders can do, what will their forwards do to us? Pat Quinn scored another just before half time but some apprehension crept in as it was the 75th minute before we got the third. Peter Cormack scored it and now we were really going for it to finish them off. But also at the back of your mind you knew an Italian side were always dangerous on the counter-attack. Then I got the fourth coming in at the back post to meet Alex Scott's cross perfectly. I headed it down just a couple of inches inside the post and Colin Stein wrapped it up with a late fifth goal.

But our luck wasn't to hold up in the next round against Leeds United who were a bogey for us on more than one occasion. Don Revie's team had some great players, but they were a cynical side. They won 1-0 at Elland Road but we pressed them hard and were unlucky to lose Colin Stein who got some really harsh treatment. The return is remembered for the controversial four-step rule decision. Colin Stein had put us level after just six minutes, but we couldn't get another. Then late in the second half Willie Wilson took more than four steps trying to get round Mick Jones to punt the ball up the park. Willie was trying to get rid of the ball as quickly as possible as we were going for the winner, but referee Clive Thomas whistled. From the free kick Jack Charlton headed the equaliser and we were out. You could say Hibs' style was a complete contrast to the Leeds team of that time who went on to win the Fairs Cup that season.

The next season we were back in Europe and beat Olympia of Yugoslavia and Lokomotiv Leipzig of East Germany easily. Then came another major contest against Hamburg of West Germany. They had

Alan McGraw and I welcome Danish centre half John Madsen (centre) to Easter Road in 1966.

World Cup finalists in their team like Uwe Seeler, but we played well to hold them to only a one-goal lead in the Volksparkstadion. Our luck ran out at home as three goals were disallowed. Joe McBride scored two that counted and then Joe Davis missed a penalty. Seeler scored one for them so they got through on the away goals rule. There were another couple of strange features about that game. Their keeper Ozcan was allowed to wear a green jersey despite our protests. Also we had been told to watch out for their left winger Dorfill, but when the team ran out we couldn't spot him. Then someone pointed out it must be the completely bald guy in their team. We hadn't realised our friend Dorfill wore a wig.

Our travel with Hibs was not limited to Europe and we went on close season tours in Bob Shankly's time to North America and Africa. When I was manager of Hibs our close-season tour was to Stornoway, which gives you some idea of how far things had slipped at Easter Road. At the end of the 1966/67 season we were part of a North American tournament, and although we were based in Toronto we played in Dallas, Houston, San Francisco, Vancouver, Cleveland and New York. They were trying to push football in America at the time and we were

Bob Shankly's Hibs squad for our North American tour in 1967.

treated like kings. I thoroughly enjoyed it and I roomed with Jimmy
O'Rourke on these trips. As well as the laughs you got, Jimmy and I
used to put in a bit of sight-seeing. We were in San Francisco at the
height of the hippy period and visited Haight Ashbury. In Dallas we
went to the Dealey Plaza where Kennedy was shot, and in New York we
played in the Yankee stadium.

Six weeks were too long for the competition and we deliberately took
it easy against Stoke City so we would get eliminated and return home
early.

One incident that does stick in my mind is when we were coming off
the pitch after playing Montreal Italia, and a guy came up to me and
said, 'You come from Craigmillar, don't you?' It was a lad called Tommy
Barrat from the old neighbourhood. Craigmillar folk seem to turn up
everywhere! When we went to Nigeria, my brother told me he knew a
guy who worked there. I forgot all about it until I was sitting in my hotel
room in Lagos and there was a knock on the door. I opened it and this
guy says, 'You're Pat Stanton, aren't you? I know your brother.' It also
happened when I was in Melbourne with Celtic and another boy I knew
from Craigmillar called up the hotel and came round for a chat about
the 'auld country'. About the only place I never bumped into anyone
from Craigmillar was in Albania, but that was probably because they
were all in jail.

While we were in Nigeria it was the Hibs team that nearly ended up in
jail. It was at the time of the Biafran civil war and we were accused of
being British mercenaries. After we struggled in our first game Bob

Bella Napoli! I head the fourth goal past the young Italian keeper who went on to do not too badly in the game. You might have heard of him — Dino Zoff (1967).

Shankly told us: 'No wonder they thought you were mercenaries as you never looked like footballers.'

These were very enjoyable days at Easter Road and I appreciated the good aspects of life as a footballer. We missed out a couple of times on winning something. In 1965 we reached the semi-final of the League Cup against Celtic. It went to a replay where we crashed 4-0 and John McNamee was sent off. Big John made a move for referee Bobby Davidson so I grabbed him round the neck but the big man just kept walking, dragging me along with him. Luckily he saw reason and stopped just in time. Three seasons later we met Celtic again, this time in the League Cup final. It was delayed till March 1969 because of the fire at Hampden and again we lost by four goals, the score this time 6-2. It was a great disappointment. Although Celtic were European champions, we let ourselves down badly.

That season we slipped to twelfth in the league and a sign of my frustration at the way things were going was when I was sent off for the first time against St Johnstone. I tried to go round their man Bill McGarry and he blocked me so I foolishly kicked him. Eight Hibs players were sent off around that time which makes the Rangers team of recent seasons look like choirboys. But we were not a dirty team, and it was more a matter of frustration as we were one of the few teams that played open attacking football, apart from Celtic. But they had Stein and the power of being an Old Firm club behind them. Bob Shankly's faith in achieving something with us had gone and he resigned early in the 1969/70 season.

The new man for the job was once again a contrast to his predecessor. Willie McFarlane was an extrovert character and his enthusiasm paid off straight away: we shot to the top of the league by beating Celtic, Rangers and Hearts all away from home. We beat Rangers 3-1 at Ibrox with Willie switching numbers and playing Peter Marinello through the middle. Peter got two goals that day, which was just another step on his road out of Easter Road. I don't know if Willie got the backing from the board he deserved or not, but there was continual turmoil at this time. Peter Marinello was sold to Arsenal just in time for the New Year's game against Hearts. I don't know why they sold Peter then as he wasn't ready to go and he became a victim of the media as they tried to create another George Best. At that time I remember watching the nine o'clock news and Peter was on it arriving in London. It showed how the whole thing had got out of proportion and I had a feeling things wouldn't turn out well for him. Peter Cormack was sent off in the New Year derby, which was a sign of his frustration, but soon he moved on to Nottingham Forest. It was around this time that I put in a transfer request of my own. I was fed up with the talk of people leaving all the time and the team getting broken up, but reconsidered when I was reassured things would get better. There were signs of a new team emerging. I didn't want to leave Hibs but if you're too loyal you get taken for granted. I was to learn that lesson even more in seasons to come, but then my heart was at Easter Road.

Willie McFarlane brought in his new men as every manager does. Arthur Duncan was a good replacement for Peter Marinello and you knew we had one advantage in keeping him as he looked nothing like George Best. Arthur was a great laugh and you knew he would always give all he had. Some players you just accept certain things from that you would not from others and Arthur was one of these. The way he hit his crosses we used to think he had spotted a pickpocket in the crowd. Another solid buy was Jim Black at centre half who would team up with

Here I outjump Jack Charlton of Leeds at Elland Road as Eric Stevenson looks on. Although I'm not particularly tall, I was always good in the air and could outjump players a lot bigger than myself.

John Blackley who had started coming through about the same time as Peter Marinello. Another promising player emerging was John Brownlie, and Willie McFarlane brought in Erich Schaedler from his former club Stirling Albion. In his debut we were playing Gornik Zabre and the first thing he did was mistime a tackle and hit Peter Cormack who was carried off. We could see the Poles looking at each other. If this is what he does to his own players, what will he do to us? When you played beside Erich you had to be alert.

Willie McFarlane was especially good with young players and maybe youth coaching would have been his strongest point. His days at Easter Road were numbered when the new board took over. Tom Hart bought out Willie Harrower in the summer of 1970 and another era was starting at Easter Road. I have the feeling Tom had his eyes already set on Eddie Turnbull who was succeeding at Aberdeen. But when Willie left a couple of months after Tom Hart took over, Dave Ewing the coach filled in but only really as an interim manager.

Davie Ewing filled the manager's post at Easter Road for only six months and was installed just before the Hibs v Liverpool UEFA Cup tie, hardly the best time to make a change. However, club policy at Easter Road has never followed the most logical of patterns. We had got so far in the UEFA Cup due to easy wins over Malmo of Sweden and Guimares of Portugal, but we lost both home and away ties to Liverpool.

The two bright spots to Dave's period in charge were the cup run and Joe Baker's return to Easter Road. As a lad Joe had been my hero just like half the schoolboys in Edinburgh at that time. His first game was against Eddie Turnbull's Aberdeen who were on a run, not having let in a goal for thirteen weeks. Joe turned out in white boots that day to a great reception from the crowd. Bobby Clark was in top form in Aberdeen's goal, but I had the honour of breaking his record and Joe got the winner. Not long after that I put an own goal past Bobby in an international against Portugal and Bobby yelled at me as he picked the ball out of the net: 'Hey, Stanton, how is it you always score against me?'

It was clear that Joe Baker was well past his best, but it was a nice touch that he could come back for his swansong at Easter Road. The cup semi-final that season against Rangers turned into a bit of a farce. The first game was a really messy affair and after it Dave Ewing was set up by the press. His comment 'Rangers are rubbish' was overheard from an open dressing-room door and taken out of context by a reporter. If it hadn't been Rangers it would never have been mentioned, but obviously the reporter thought he could stir things up a bit. Although Jimmy O'Rourke scored for us in the replay, we didn't put up a good show and Rangers won 2-1. Dave Ewing left soon after in the close season. He had been popular with the players, a big no-nonsense type of person, but he returned down south, realising his appointment had been a stop gap measure.

CHAPTER SIX

Turnbull's Tornadoes

WHEN Tom Hart took over, we were confident that now the only way was up. We could see he had been a success in business and felt he would bring that touch to running Easter Road. Also Tom Hart was a Hibs man through and through, which cannot be said for every club chairman. To many it is a status symbol or they are in it for what they can get out of the club, but you knew Tom Hart was there because he wanted to make Hibs a great club again. Tom Hart thought big and nothing was too good for Hibs. So he went for the best man available to manage Hibs. Eddie Turnbull had won the cup at Aberdeen and had established them as the main rivals of the Old Firm in Scotland. After Eddie's playing career he had been trainer at Easter Road before moving on to Queen's Park and Aberdeen. One thing about Eddie Turnbull no one could ever dispute was he had forgotten more about football than most people ever know. He could read the game well, tactically was very astute and had sound ideas on training. But the area he fell down in was man management. Eddie was a gruff sort and would have won no prizes at a charm school. He didn't have much rapport with the players and belonged to the school that believed you should rule by fear. There is more to management than that, and it is no secret that Eddie and I did not get on too well.

But when Hibs failed to win trophies or titles over the next few seasons I would not blame Eddie. It was the players that let him down though I'm sure he made a mistake in breaking up his first team too early. He thought we were never going to really do it and changes were needed, but he should have been a bit more patient. I was also to fall out with him later on when I felt I was made a scapegoat for a general drop in form in 1975. I was never told to my face that I was getting dropped, which was the least I thought I deserved. I paid the price for my

I hook one in much to Colin Stein's delight as the Hearts defence is spread all over the place. Jim Cruikshank looks as if he is following up to net a rebound. (1968).

versatility over that period and got little thanks for it. When I left Hibs I thought I had done a good job for Eddie as a player, but I never got a word of thanks from him or any good luck for the future.

However, even Eddie had his moments and one of his best was his famous put-down of Alan Gordon. I think Eddie felt a bit insecure, especially with someone like Alan who was well educated and an accountant by training. Alan used to regularly question something at the tactics talk and a lot of it was solely to wind up Eddie. One day Alan started as usual, but this time Eddie was ready and cut him short: 'The trouble with you, Gordon, is your brains are in your f****** heid!'

The Hibs team under Turnbull was to go on and eclipse the side of the previous few seasons. As I've said, I enjoyed playing some of my best football over that period and had won international honours and played in European football. Just before Turnbull arrived I was awarded the Scottish Football Writers' Player of the Year award. Of course I was honoured especially as Celtic reached the European Cup final that year against Feyenoord. They had beaten Leeds in a superb semi-final. So it was some honour to be selected ahead of players from a great Celtic team who had reached the European Cup final.

Hibernian squad: season 1968-69.

That award did mean something to me, although I am not a great man for them. If you walked into my house there is nothing on the walls or the sideboards to tell you I was ever a footballer. I think you can hang on to the past too much. I also realise the luck involved in medals and awards and they are often not a true reflection of what you were as a footballer. I know some exceptional players who won hardly anything and never got a cap, but I can think of quite a few Old Firm players, particularly from Rangers, who were very ordinary yet have medals and caps they would never have got if they had been at another club.

Meanwhile Eddie Turnbull was to create a great team that won a major trophy, the League Cup, and two Drybrough Cups. He was to make three quick signings that were very important — Jim Herriot in goal, Alex Edwards in midfield and Alan Gordon up front. Both Jim and Alex were characters in their own right, Jim with his warpaint, the soot he rubbed under his eyes to stop glare from the sun, and his mazy dribbles out of the box. Wee 'Mickey' was a terrific player who suffered for the amount of stick he had to take from players who were hardly fit to lace his boots. He got done by referees time and again for retaliation. Many people wrongly thought he was undisciplined, but you only had to watch him in training to realise that was nonsense. Alex was a key player in the team and when he received some of his very severe suspensions the whole team suffered. Alan Gordon was another one of

Bobby Brown collects me for the Scotland squad to play Eire as I leave an SFA disciplinary meeting in 1969. I was fined £30 and suspended for six days after being sent off against St Johnstone.

those former Hearts players who found his way to Easter Road, but in his case it was via Dundee United. Alan was an elegant player who was great in the air and was the perfect foil for a bustling forward like Jimmy O'Rourke.

Peter Cormack and I had just been selected to play for the Scottish League against England in 1969.

Another astute buy was Bertie Auld. Bertie was another who fitted that much over-used word 'character'. A player with great skill, Bertie was a bit flier than wee Mickey as he used to get his retaliation in first. We played Middlesbrough in a pre-season friendly and we all looked forward to the duel between Bertie and Nobby Stiles who was finishing his career with them. The former Manchester United man had a reputation as one of the toughest players in football, but that didn't bother Bertie. There was a bit of early sparring and then Bertie teased

Hibs team 1968. Back (left to right) John Blackley, Joe Davis, Billy Simpson, Jim Black, Thomson Allan, Gordon Marshall, Pat Stanton, Chris Shevlane, John Madsen.
Front (left to right) Colin Grant, Alex Scott, Peter Cormack, Peter Marinello, Jimmy O'Rourke, Joe McBride, Willie Hunter, Eric Stevenson and Tom McNiven.

Nobby into making a lunge at him. Usually in these situations Nobby really crunched someone, but Bertie had set his bait. He skipped into the tackle as Stiles came flying in at him. The next thing you knew Bertie was picking himself up from a crumpled heap and brushing a speck of dirt off his shorts, keen to get on with the game. Meanwhile Nobby lay on the deck and on came the trainer and Nobby was carried off.

Meanwhile Eddie Turnbull had to think on his feet that season. He did well to turn around a team that had been in turmoil and we finished fourth in the league and reached the cup final. Everyone was on a high about reaching Hampden, but we ended up trounced 6-1 by Celtic. That was a sore one. We were level 1-1 at half time as Alan Gordon equalised Billy McNeill's early goal, but Dixie Deans ran riot in the second half along with Jimmy Johnstone. I felt we let a lot of people down that day and couldn't face going into the reception at the North British hotel after the game. One thing I was certain of on the bus coming back from Hampden was that we would get our revenge.

With the Scotland team at Largs 1969. Back (left to right) Trainer Tom McNiven, Davy Hay, Bobby Moncur, Jim Cruikshank, Ronnie McKinnon, Pat Stanton, John Greig and manager Bobby Brown.
Front Jimmy Johnstone, Willie Carr, Colin Stein, John O'Hare and Willie Johnston. As usual Bud's forgotten his shoes.

We didn't have long to wait as we won the Drybrough Cup at the start of the next season. In the Drybrough Cup they experimented with an offside line by the 18-yard line which made it really hard on midfield players. If you played a whole season like that you would be burying some of them at the end of it. In the semi-final we hammered Rangers, who had just won the European Cup Winners' Cup, 3-0 and then went 3-0 up against Celtic in the final. They pulled back to 3-3, but in extra time Jimmy O'Rourke and Arthur Duncan won the match for us. We had had something to prove to ourselves and had done it. Now both our league form and performance in Europe were really to take off.

We were in the European Cup Winners' Cup courtesy of our appearance in the final. Celtic were then in the process of notching up their nine league wins in a row. So many people remember our game with Sporting Lisbon when we hammered them 6-1 at Easter Road that season, but it was a pity nobody saw our first leg in Lisbon. I say that

Up before the beaks: John Blackley and I can manage a smile before we appear before an S.F.A. disciplinary committee when I was Hibs manager.

because it was the best performance I ever played in with a Hibs team. That may surprise a lot of people. Some would choose the League Cup final, others a Drybrough Cup performance, and then again there were many other European ties to pick from, or our 7-0 win on New Year's Day 1973 at Tynecastle. But that night in Lisbon everything gelled and we put on a perfect team performance. Sporting were a very good team

Greensleeves were not Hearts' delight when I scored this goal in 1972. Alan Anderson and Dave Clunie look on. The empty terrace in the background was due to work on that superb piece of architecture which is now known as the seated enclosure. In those days it was The Shed.

and they had a massive support of over 100,000 behind them that night. Even though they won 2-1 they knew they were out of it. The crowd as well had started off roaring them on, but they quietened down as the game progressed. Although we weren't thumping the ball into the back of the net, we were playing beautifully controlled football. Everybody in the team was spot on. We came off the pitch totally satisfied. Even in games you win well you realise you made certain mistakes and you got breaks in your favour or the opposition made errors. But that night we were as close to perfect as you could get. I don't know if it had anything to do with the purple strips we wore for the one and only time. Also there may be something in the air in Lisbon as Scottish clubs seem to do well there.

In the return at Easter Road Sporting went one goal in front, but they knew, and we knew they knew, that it was just going to be a matter of time before we took them apart. In the second half Jimmy O'Rourke scored one of his six hat-tricks that season as we went on to win 6-1.

Our next European tie was against FC Besa of Albania. We won 7-1 at home, but the return leg in Albania was something else. I had been to Russia and Czechoslovakia with Scotland but I had never seen anything like this before. When we arrived at the airport it was just a few huts,

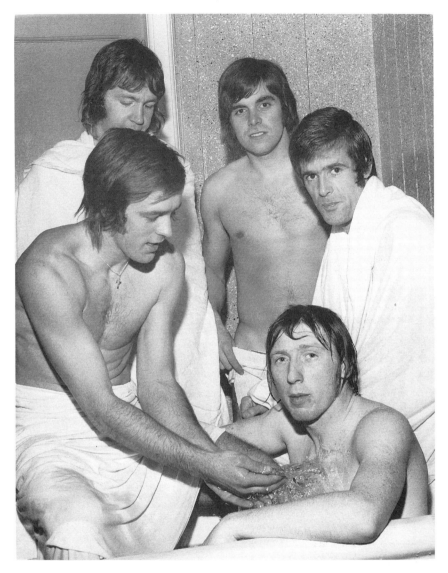

Erich Schaedler makes sure John Brownlie keeps his cool as John Blackley, Alex Edwards and I relax in the steam room at Portobello Baths (1972).

and I remember there was this wee porter watching the cases. The next time I saw him he was serving up the soup in the hotel. Here he was posing as a waiter, but he had obviously been detailed to spy on us. Another classic in Albania was when we went to check out the pitch. Someone noticed the crossbar was too low so the referee asked their officials to do something about it. So instead of erecting new posts they dug a trench right along the goal line. Luckily we had a lot in hand and

For once Eddie Turnbull is smiling. We had just won the League Cup against Celtic and received a tremendous reception when we arrived back at the North British Hotel. He probably still has the SMT rug he borrowed off the bus.

drew 1-1 with Besa. The round before they had played a team from free and easy Copenhagen. I don't know what they must have made of it, but it's a wonder the whole team had not defected.

However, we still had a lot to learn in Europe as we were well beaten 3-0 in Yugoslavia by Hadjuk Split after winning 4-2 at Easter Road. Eddie Turnbull pointed out how we still had a lot to learn about European football after the home game. We were four goals up when we lost two late goals. We fell for the classic sucker punch in European football where you must guard against losing any goals at home at all cost. Also by that time our season had begun to fall away. Maybe we peaked too soon, but our best form was in the League Cup and in the league in December.

By the time we got to the knockout stage in the league cup we were unbeatable. We beat Dundee United 5-1 at Tannadice and then went to Broomfield. The Airdrie match was real end-to-end stuff and Arthur went a wee bit haywire that night. At times he was coming in from the right wing so it meant he had the whole pitch to keep the ball in and some of the time I think it even ended up in the net. John Brownlie also showed his form in that game which was to prove vital in the semi-finals against Rangers. Brownlie was a great player. A good, strong tackler, he was the best attacking full back I have seen. If he hadn't broken his leg, there's no saying what he would have done in the game. In the semi-final John, Alex Edwards and I linked up particularly well on the right and John broke through to shoot in off the bar. Although we won only 1-0, the score belied how good we were that night.

We were very confident we would win the final and should have really hammered Celtic. If it had been six for us they would have got off lightly. Eddie Turnbull never mentioned the previous cup final defeat, but then again none of us needed any reminding. As we set off to Hampden that day a wee laddie threw a brick through the bus window as it went up Easter Road and we had to sit there freezing all the way to Glasgow. Somebody suggested we should do that every week as at least when we got to Hampden we were wide awake. This was our chance for revenge and we were raring to go.

There was a great Hibs support at Hampden that day and we felt good at half-time although we were still level. Then in the second half I made the breakthrough. We had a free kick just outside the Celtic box. It wasn't preplanned, but I walked across the back of the Celtic wall and nobody went with me. Alex saw me and chipped the ball over the wall. As I collected it I began to move away from goal. A lot of people have told me they thought I had lost my chance, but I knew what I was doing. I just wanted to get another yard or so clear for my chance. If I had played it right away I would have possibly hit a defender, so I was making sure I got a clear angle before I stuck it past Evan Williams.

We were now sure we would win and I helped create the second. Again it came from the right. In fact it was just about the first time I had been up the right wing in my life, so when Alex slipped the ball to me I thought I had better get rid of it quickly! I flighted it across and there was Jimmy running through to bullet it in with his head. Maybe it was only fitting that the two oldest Hibbies in the team should have got the goals.

We got a superb reception when we got back to Edinburgh with thousands packing into Princes Street. I was so glad we had made it up to the fans after losing the cup final six months before. I would still have liked it to have been the cup rather than the League Cup. That is not meant as any disrespect to the competition and we had played with real style in the previous rounds. During this period Easter Road was really buzzing and we were not the only people who thought we would go all the way that season. Our next match was a home game against Ayr United and we were conscious of not making it an anti-climax for the

The final whistle goes at the League Cup final and we trot over to salute the Hibs support. Alan Gordon is alongside me while Alex Cropley tries to hitch a lift from Jim Black. Arthur Duncan has his mind on other things. (1972).

fans as so many times a team gets a great result and the next game is a let down. Well, we excelled ourselves, winning 8-1, and Ally McLeod their manager at the time described Hibs as playing like the great Real Madrid side. What was so good about that side was so many could get goals and everyone was in on the act at that time — the front three of Alan, Jimmy and Arthur, Mickey, myself and Alec Cropley in midfield, and John Brownlie would join in from the back. Sometimes I even thought Jim Herriot would get on the score sheet as he came dribbling out of the box.

We were then held to a draw away to Celtic, then beat Aberdeen 3-2, but that game again was a case of where we should have scored ten. Somewhere along the line I knew someone was really going to catch it from us and it just happened to be Hearts on New Year's Day. I have always enjoyed playing at Tynecastle. I liked the pitch and the atmosphere was always good for derby games. Hearts were going well at the time, lying third in the league. But that day we could not be stopped. I also think Kenny Garland had a good game in Hearts' goal that day and was not really to blame for any of the goals. I remembered when we were four up after ten minutes against Hearts at Tynecastle in a derby game in 1965 when Eric Stevenson and Jimmy got two each. After building such a lead we really eased off and ended up taking the mickey out of Hearts. After the game my father said we should never have done that, going about humiliating fellow professionals. I believe he was right and must say that during the 7-0 game we didn't go out to do that to the Hearts players. There is a difference when you start to turn it on and relax and enjoy yourself, which we did this time.

Jimmy opened the scoring and Alan Gordon, Arthur Duncan and Alex Cropley were the other scorers. We were five up at half time and Turnbull wanted us to go out in the second half and make an even better job of it. At times there was no satisfying Eddie Turnbull. I still believe I should have had the sixth. I drew out the keeper and slipped the ball past him, but who should slide in to get a touch as it crossed the line but O'Rourke? I have never forgiven him for it. How could he have done that to his old pal?

We were quite pleased with the result, but it was only two or three days later that the real impact of it had sunk in. It was a result that would never be forgotten and would become part of Edinburgh football folklore. The result also took us to the top of the league as we were six goals behind Celtic on goal average before the game. Now everybody thought it was our league.

But by the very next game things began to fall apart. John Brownlie broke his leg in two places and Alex Edwards retaliated by throwing the ball at Johnny Love who had been kicking him all afternoon. He got booked and received a savage eight-week suspension. This badly affected the right-side partnership I had with Alex and John. So many of our attacks were built from this area, we never fully recovered from that double blow we received. We faded badly and finished third in the league and were knocked out of the UEFA Cup by Hadjuk Split. We didn't have much luck either in the cup where after a draw at Ibrox we lost the replay 2-1 at Easter Road. Tommy McLean took a dive after John Blackley tackled him near the edge of the box and referee Bobby Davidson obliged Rangers with a penalty.

It was a very disappointing end to what had seemed such a promising season. We won the first two competitions we were in: the League Cup and Drybrough Cup. We led the league at one stage and showed dazzling form in Europe. Eddie Turnbull was embittered by it all. In some ways I don't think you can blame Eddie for thinking if we didn't do it that season, then we would never do it. The following season we played some great stuff, but before the season was over Eddie Turnbull had started breaking up the team with Jimmy O'Rourke and Alex Cropley both leaving.

We started off, as we had the season before, winning the Drybrough

I lift the League Cup at Hampden as Glasgow Lord Provost William Gray and Jim Herriot look on. (1972).

Cup again, beating Rangers in the semis and Celtic in the final 1-0. But we slipped up at Tynecastle with Hearts winning 4-1. This was one of the rare occasions Hearts beat us during my time as a player with Hibs. As I said earlier, the tide began to turn with the New Year win in 1965 when Willie Hamilton got that tremendous goal. In the next couple of seasons we got our first home win in a derby for 14 years and the next season got our first win on New Year's Day in 20 years. Even the Famous Five for some reason had a jinx when it came to playing Hearts, but throughout my playing career it worked the other way. These goals Hearts got in their 4-1 victory were the first they had scored in a derby for five years. So although it may have been hard going for Hibs fans in the last few seasons against Hearts, they have to remember the boot was on the other foot during my playing career and, if anything, we dominated Hearts far more thoroughly.

As I have said, I always enjoyed playing at Tynecastle and liked the pitch, which is more than I can say for the slope at Easter Road. It has always been one of my pet hates and I can never understand why nothing has ever been done about it. Also why is it construed as being

Reading all about it. For once I thought the papers were spot on! (1972).

an advantage for Hibs? Remember half the game you are playing uphill and no team should have to deal with that at home. I'm sure AC Milan don't play on a slope at the San Siro stadium. For the best football get the best surface available, and that is always a flat one, not some stupid slope.

We went on to win second place in the league in the 1973/74 season but one of the highlights was our UEFA cup tie with Leeds. Like the last time, the first leg was at Elland Road where we got a draw. We had played well and were looking forward to getting revenge. We threw everything at them in the return and I still cannot understand why we

I am the invisible man holding the League Cup aloft as John Blackley, sporting
a Hibs tammy, follows me through the crowd outside the North British. (1972).

didn't score. It came to penalties and I stepped forward to take the first
one, only to hit it off the post. I was the only one not to score as Alex
Cropley, John Blackley, Des Bremner and John Hazel scored for Hibs.
Billy Bremner hit in Leeds' fifth penalty off the underside of the bar.
Once again I thought we had been robbed against Leeds.

After this Eddie Turnbull made his controversial move to sign Joe
Harper from Everton for then a club record of £120,000. Obviously
Eddie thought Joe was the key to turning Hibs into a championship-
winning team. It was not to be, and the move was seen by many as the
beginning of the end of Turnbull's best Hibs team. Eddie made the
mistake a lot of managers make. He remembered Harper as he used to
be when he was first with Aberdeen and thought Joe would recreate
exactly the same performances for Hibs. Managers will have a particular
favourite who has really done the business for them and are often too
slow to see how a player can change. No one can doubt that Joe Harper

was a very good player, and when I was at Aberdeen he was their local hero. But when he came to Hibs he had slowed down and was overweight. Also a lot of disharmony crept into the team.

Jimmy O'Rourke, Alan Gordon and Arthur Duncan had scored 100 goals between them the season before, so it is difficult to see Eddie's reasoning. On paper it looked as if he had strengthened the pool, but someone had to go. At first Alan made way for Joe Harper, but soon it became clear Jimmy was the man marked down to go. This definitely did not help Joe's position as he would really have to go some now to stand in for Jimmy. He had just scored nineteen goals in fifteen games after being out the side for a while. Also Jimmy was a great favourite with the fans, not just because he was a great player with a superb attitude, but also because he was a total Hibs man.

Although we reached the League Cup final that season, it was the beginning of the end. Jimmy was to leave at the end of that season as well as Alex Cropley.

CHAPTER SEVEN

The Long Goodbye

OUR league position had improved each season since Eddie Turnbull took over, but this was not good enough as we had not won the league. In his first season 1971/72 we were fourth and reached the Cup Final. In 1972/73 we finished third and won the League Cup and the Drybrough Cup and in season 1973/74 we were second in the League and again won the Drybrough Cup. Not a bad record for some clubs, but Hibs wanted to topple Celtic as the top club in Scotland. Celtic were still a great side at the time and over this period the Lisbon Lions were being replaced by the likes of Danny McGrain, Kenny Dalglish, Lou Macari and a man who was always a thorn in our side, Dixie Deans. On top of this they were managed by Jock Stein. So in some ways it would have taken some feat to displace Celtic, with all the advantages they have as one of the Old Firm.

People forget how much the odds are stacked in the Old Firm's favour with their huge support, the natural advantage of playing semi-finals and finals in the west at Hampden and the refereeing decisions that go their way. Referees are influenced by crowds and this regularly works to the Old Firm's advantage. Both of them think they are hard done by, but this is not the case. Just ask anybody who has played for Scotland's other clubs.

Anyway in 1974/75 season we were to come close again and finished second in the league, but this time it was Rangers who won it. I don't know if it was the week in October that was the last straw for Turnbull and made him dismantle the team. But it was a really bad week where we lost twice to Celtic and were knocked out of Europe. Celtic beat us 5-0 in the League at Parkhead and scored another six against us in their 6-3 League Cup final victory the next Saturday at Hampden. On the

Wednesday in between we lost 4-2 at home to Juventus. After going behind we had pulled back to lead 2-1. Then they brought on Altafini as substitute. He was about 36 at the time and was a wee barrel with his socks at his ankles, but he showed devastating form, scoring two goals. The League Cup final on the Saturday was another painful experience: Joe Harper scored a hat trick, but still ended up on the losing side.

Alex Cropley was sold shortly after to Arsenal although as far as I know he was not wanting away. Once again it was the old story of talented young players being sold off without asking away. Eddie Turnbull had obviously decided to rebuild as we were seen to fail again, finishing second in the league. Also the Premier League was starting in the next season which also happened to be Hibs' centenary season.

Most players' attitude towards the Premier League was to give it a chance, but we didn't look forward to playing sides four times in a season. We thought we would get to know each other too well and the game might suffer from a spectator's point of view. However, it would take away the aura the Old Firm had and they would now get beaten more often. Teams would now become less intimidated about going to Parkhead or Ibrox twice a season.

Also at this time Hibs celebrated their centenary and it shows how much has changed in a decade because, to be quite frank, not a very good job was made of it. We played Derby County, the English champions, at Easter Road and there was a big do at the North British Hotel. Everybody who had been associated with the club as far back as can be remembered was invited to it, but none of the current team were. Maybe it was because it was too close to a game, but it always struck me as strange that some guys who had played two games for the reserves in 1923 were there, whereas members of the present team which had won trophies were not.

Morale was not high at Easter Road at this time, but really this was a reflection on the management. We had just finished second in the league and were in Europe. Also a club with a proud history was celebrating its centenary, but things just did not feel right. Then came the game at Montrose and my first open split with the management. We had beaten them 1-0 in the first leg of the League Cup tie, but then crashed 3-1 at Links Park. I was not playing particularly well at the time, but not many of the other players could have been too happy with their form against Montrose that night. I was also playing further forward than I had for a long time and wasn't happy about that either. At that stage in my career I shouldn't have needed to play in midfield, but I suffered because I had put the needs of the club before my own needs.

Looking back now, I can see that's not too clever a thing to do because you get no thanks for it. I should have been playing at the back by now, but I was still being asked to do jobs I wasn't suited to any more. But one of the biggest disappointments on this occasion was that Turnbull didn't tell me to my face I was being dropped.

Another player told me. He had overheard something and had let me know. Then as we got ready for training, one of the ground staff handed me a 'possibles' bib. I knew then what this player had warned me about was true. I had been at Easter Road long enough to get told to my face, but the staff were not brave enough to tell me. Even a 20-year-old deserves an explanation when he's dropped.

What had annoyed me most about it all was the way it was done. Then when I went and asked for a rest as I felt jaded, my request was turned down and I was sent to play in a reserve match at Dunfermline. It was then I sent in a written transfer request.

We had already beaten Liverpool 1-0 in the UEFA Cup at home thanks to a Joe Harper goal, and John Brownlie missed a penalty. But after I had been dropped to play St Johnstone I was still out for the return tie at Anfield. Alex Edwards put us ahead, but we lost out to three identical headers by John Toshack at the back post. As I sat on the bench it made me even more frustrated as I thought I could have done a good job marking Toshack in these positions as I've always rated myself as good in the air. I felt thoroughly fed up and broke the curfew back at the hotel that night along with John Blackley. We were fined £25 but I didn't really care. Other players were sympathetic to my situation, but you have to get on with your own game and look after yourself.

I had very mixed feelings at this time because of the way I felt about Hibs, but I wasn't happy with the management. We were never far off just doing it and I have often felt a bit more subtlety in the way the team was handled could have produced the results needed to clinch trophies. Over this period I got great support from the fans who had also written into the papers on my behalf. The Easter Road fans were always very good to me and I was lucky in this way during my career. Even during my short spell at Celtic the fans were very good to me.

However, after missing four games I was back in the team against Celtic at Parkhead. We were leading 2-0 before the game was abandoned with less than ten minutes to go because of fog. Celtic managed to get a draw in the replay, but I would lay you any odds that game would not have been abandoned if the score had been reversed at

Kicking cash for charity at The Snuff Box in Holyrood Road. Jimmy O'Rourke could count it all before it hit the floor. (1973).

the time. Now I was back in the team, but I was still played in an attacking midfield role just behind the forwards. Although my preference has always been for the back, I still banged in a few goals. Maybe it was because I felt I had something to prove to the management for dropping me in the first place. It was at this time I scored my famous 94th-minute goal at Tynecastle.

We were one behind, but had most of the play in the second half. We were pushing hard for a goal as they hadn't beaten us for a long time. The Hearts fans had started to whistle for the referee to blow and we were aware we were heading into extra time as the crowds were moving towards the exit. But we had enough in us to keep plugging away. I moved forward and started to make a run into the box and saw a cross come in from the right. I got up well to it and headed it in. Straight away I looked at the linesman as there was a hint of offside about it but his flag stayed down. By the time the centre was taken the referee whistled immediately for full time. Our fans probably took more out of it than us as they saw it as Hibs snatching a draw. But we were annoyed we had not won as we were the better team.

Today I still get Hearts fans bringing that goal up to me and after it the *Daily Record* journalist Alistair Nichol made the point that I would score others, but that is the one most people would remember me scoring. Before the days of all-day pub licences, when the bars didn't open till five o'clock a couple of old Hearts fans in Portobello pulled me up about it saying, 'Remember that goal you scored, Pat, when the pubs had opened?' I knew it was a long second half, but surely we hadn't been still playing at five o'clock!

I continued to hit quite good form and soon after got both goals in a 2-1 win over Rangers. We went on to finish third in the Premier League, but I knew the writing was on the wall for me at Easter Road. I was dissatisfied at how things were going for me at Easter Road and the experience at the start of the 1975/76 season had left me with a sour taste. I realised that I was getting on a bit and at that time I thought I might end up with a team like St Johnstone or St Mirren. I also knew I was no longer really wanted by Hibs although I felt I still had something to give. In a pre-season tour of Ireland I was sitting on the team bus and the song 'I heard it through the Grapevine' was on the radio. I felt there was a message somewhere in there for me. It occurred to me that this would be my last tour anywhere with Hibs and my days with them were numbered. In some ways I didn't care any more. Football is a hard game and players move on all the time and that is it. You learn to live with it.

The rot at Hibs at that time had started to set in with Joe Harper's arrival, although Joe himself cannot be blamed for it. It did look a good buy at the time, but things began to go wrong. Also when players like Cropley, Blackley and Brownlie began to move on, their replacements were not of the same calibre. Likewise splinter groups began to appear with people hanging around in cliques. After certain games the defence would blame the attack and vice versa. It's a bad sign when no one accepts responsibility and it's a bad habit players have when things start to go wrong. It is always someone else's fault. If this is happening, the

Bonnyrigg Rose head off to the Junior Cup Final with me far right at the very back. I was invited along as a former player.

only solution is to clear out the players responsible, because if it raises its head once it will happen again.

Easter Road was not a happy place at this time and when I looked back I could remember better days. I was back on the substitutes' bench and my last game for Hibs was to come in the League Cup when we beat St Johnstone 9-2. With three minutes to go George Stewart, a recent arrival at Hibs, was substituted and on I went. You could have taken off seven others with him and Hibs would still have won, but I have always been grateful to George for these three minutes.

Around that time I played well in a reserve game against Celtic with Bobby Lennox, Andy Ritchie and Danny McGrain up against me and that performance might have reinforced Jock Stein's notion to sign me.

The move to Celtic was really to take me by surprise but I had absolutely no hesitation in taking it. However, when I actually left Easter Road it was still on a sour note. The deal had been done; I went in to collect my boots and Tom McNiven was the only person there. I was willing to let bygones be bygones and hoped the club would pull itself back into shape. This was a good break for me, but I still wished Hibs well. Tom wished me all the best, but that was it. Nobody from the Hibs staff picked up a phone and thanked me for my contribution and wished me all the best for the future. Walking out the door I felt like a trialist who had been a failure. I thought then that when you considered the effort I had put into Hibs for over fifteen years, it showed them up for what they were.

CHAPTER EIGHT

A Taste of Paradise

I SUPPOSE there was more than a touch of irony in the way I was to return to Easter Road less than a year later to win the league with Celtic. I took a lot of satisfaction from what had happened to me that season. I had been discarded by Hibs as a player who was past it, yet here was I picking up a league and Scottish Cup medal, the two top honours in the Scottish game which had eluded me in all my years at Easter Road. Never for a moment did I think that would happen, as I prepared for season 1976/77 sitting on a substitutes' bench on Hibs' pre-season tour of Ireland. It was also nice to know that the top man in the Scottish game, Jock Stein, still valued my services. It was a great way to end my playing career and I think I did more than a good job for them.

The day of the transfer, I was supposed to be playing for the reserves that night against Hearts at Tynecastle. I was about to go out in the morning with my wife Margaret when the phone rang just as we left the house. I almost left it, but decided to go back in. It was Eddie Turnbull on the line: 'I have Mr Stein here. He'd like to talk to you.' Jock came on and said, 'I'm here at Easter Road and I'd like to speak to you. Would you like to come to Celtic?' There was not a moment's hesitation. Yes, of course I would. We agreed to meet out on the Maybury Road between the Barnton Hotel and the Glasgow Road. I was elated driving out there. I didn't know how it was going to turn out but it was a chance I couldn't turn down. Most players at my stage took a step down, but here was I joining Scotland's most successful club.

I pulled in alongside his car and got in beside him. He was very matter-of-fact and said if I came through the next day and signed up I would be playing on Saturday. At this juncture I told him I hadn't played for two or three weeks, but he brushed this aside: 'Don't worry,

The wearing of the green. I don the hoops as I sign for Celtic in 1977.

you'll be ready for Saturday.' I then asked who the game was against. He scratched his head, thought for a second or two and said, 'What's their name again? Oh aye, it's that team Rangers.' I had never seen an Old Firm game before, but Stein knew once again how to really gee me up. If I wasn't ready for this one, then I shouldn't be playing for Celtic.

I signed on and I remember going into training on the Friday. It was a warm day and the lads had heavy tracksuits on, but when Stein came out he told them to take them off as he didn't want them working up too much of a sweat before the big game. It was just one of these little things, but it was another example of Stein's great attention to detail. I relished the atmosphere and wasn't bothered about it being an Old Firm game. It was a 2-2 draw and I played well in midfield. In my second game at Tannadice I was also in midfield, but this was just a stopgap measure, and from then on I played at the back. Stein told me, 'You're here to stop goals.' At Easter Road even when I played at the back I had to go up for free kicks and corners, but in all my time at Celtic I don't think I crossed the halfway line once. I just stayed back and made sure nothing happened at the back and helped the players around me. Roy Aitken was just a laddie then and Tommy Burns sometimes used to play at left back. That season we only lost four games and won the league comfortably. When I also got my Scottish Cup medal after beating Rangers Jimmy O'Rourke phoned me up on the Sunday morning to tell me: 'Well done! That's you won all three now.' It was a gesture I really appreciated and I'll always remember Jimmy for doing that.

Lots of players go through their whole career without getting anything. Even with Hibs you would see Celtic and Rangers players winning medals and it would get to the stage you would say to yourself, 'Can I win things?' Then you do it: you realise you can. I was in my 30s now so I probably appreciated it a bit more.

At Celtic Park they certainly know how to make you feel welcome and I loved the big crowds and the big club atmosphere. At Hibs, crowds were up and down, but at Celtic you responded to atmosphere and you didn't have the problem of having to create your own atmosphere. Sometimes Hibs' performances suffered because of this. I know some people say you should be professional enough to overcome that, but it's harder than you think. It is a great advantage the Old Firm have; ask their players how they would feel about playing in front of 5,000 or 35,000.

It was also great to be back with Jock Stein. I always felt my relationship was a bit special with him and it was great seeing him at work. One time against Motherwell we were struggling a bit at Parkhead while Rangers had a vital game elsewhere. So at half time the Big Man is giving us a bit of stick, when the old guy who brought round the half time scores puts his head round the door. Stein grabbed the sheet from him and said, 'Look at that. Rangers are getting beaten and you cannae beat this lot here.' Sure enough we went back out to make sure we took full advantage of Rangers' slip. When we got back in, the full-time scores

Bobby McKean of Rangers takes a tumble, but, honest, I hadn't touched him. (1976).

were getting touted around. I turned to Andy Lynch: 'What did he say the score was with Rangers at half time?' It had been 1-0 to Rangers, who had gone on to win. Stein's fib had had exactly the right effect. If we'd known Rangers were winning we might have got too bothered thinking about that, but as we thought they were losing, here was our chance to go further ahead of them. He was a master of psychology and knew what would motivate you.

I also got on very well with the players at Parkhead such as Dalglish, McGrain, Aitken, Lynch, Glavin, Doyle and Alfie Conn. There was always the big club attitude about the place and they had a tremendous support. It didn't matter who Celtic played, they always fancied their chances. It was great playing with people like Dalglish. When you were hitting a through ball you wouldn't see Dalglish at first and then you would take another quick glance before you hit and then he would show. He always knew when to move and had perfect timing.

Stein was just the same as at Easter Road. He knew when to give you a hard time and when to encourage you. He left most of the post mortems to early the next week. He would make you aware of your mistakes just enough so you would think about it over the weekend. This gave you the chance to see where you had gone wrong.

My first return to Easter Road ended in a 1-1 draw, but the next time was when we clinched the league. We needed one point and we won 1-0. I remember one occasion when Arthur Duncan was up to his usual tricks and collided into Peter Latchford. I pushed Arthur away right in the box and the North Stand leapt to their feet booing at me. I turned towards them as if to admonish them saying, 'That'll do now!' When the match was over the ground staff at Easter Road congratulated me, but Eddie Turnbull said nothing to me and neither did any of the directors. I was satisfied and my thoughts flashed back to when I had walked out with my boots under my arm less than a year before and here I was now with a league medal. There was further irony when I was to come back and win the league with Aberdeen at Easter Road when I was assistant manager there.

Another satisfying thing was that I was playing well in a position I felt I should have been playing in for years at Easter Road. But that league medal at Easter Road was not to be the end of the season. We were to face Rangers in the first cup final to be televised live. Andy Lynch scored an early penalty and in the second half we had two or three good chances to finish them off, but we did not. So in the last five minutes we were lashing the ball anywhere. I now had three medals, but was to miss out on a Glasgow Cup one as I was injured. I also picked up a booking as well as a medal that day. Wee Tommy McLean pulled me down and I squared up to him a bit. Then a few minutes later I pulled Derek Parlane down as he went up the touchline. The referee Bob Valentine booked me, but it wasn't for that foul. He was booking me for what I had done a minute before. But it's something you just have to accept; referees are only human. Well, at least some of them are.

Bobby Clark (back row, third from the right) and I were called up as over age players for Scotland Under 21s against Czechoslovakia in Pilsen in 1978. Under these bouffant hair does lurk a few well kent faces.

It's only when you're playing for either of the Old Firm you get some idea of how important these games are and the full extent of what it means. I stayed in Edinburgh and was content to go through on a Saturday, pick up a couple of points for Celtic and drive back home. Rangers have always had a tradition of players from the east like Willie Woodburn, John Greig, Sandy Jardine, and Graeme Souness today, but very few Celtic players come from the Edinburgh area. As far as I know Ronnie Simpson and I are the only recent ones apart from the Hibs players Celtic nicked back in 1888. I used to get a bit of mickey taking from these uncouth Glaswegians about my good Edinburgh habit of using the word 'ken'. Every day I would walk in to Celtic Park and wee Johnny Doyle would say, 'How ye doing, Pat, ken!'

Everywhere you went at Parkhead you were exposed to Celtic people, whether it was the guy cutting the grass or the women serving the tea. At other clubs it's just people filling a job, but at Celtic they're supporters too. Jimmy Kennedy, for instance, who looked after the tickets, used to play for Celtic and you knew he would run through a brick wall for them. That was the environment you were exposed to.

One game against Rangers the actual match was almost a sideshow. Peter Latchford was injured, the crowd was spilling onto the track and big Stein was out the dug-out ushering them all back in. Meanwhile Roy Aitken was belting down the park and sticking one in for us. It was

Bobby Lennox, Andy Lynch, Johnny Doyle, Paul Wilson and myself pose with our children and Jock Stein with his grandson at Parkhead. It is sad to think both Jock and Johnny are no longer with us.

superb theatre and in a way I thought it would have been nice to have had ten years of this. But I had great days at Easter Road and the only thing that coloured it was the way I left. There had been talk earlier in my career that Celtic were interested in signing me, but it never went further than that.

It never really arose that Rangers would be interested in me for obvious reasons, but it wouldn't have bothered me in the slightest if they had tried to sign me. Of course now things have changed with the signing of Maurice Johnston. It's the breakthrough that so many people in Scotland have been waiting for. I wish the lad all the best. He's a top-class player and should do well. At the time of writing Johnston has just moved to Ibrox, but if he goes on to score the goals he is capable of, that should do the business in shutting up the bigots.

People have always said the first Catholic who played for Rangers would not be able to stand the pressure. Well, in some ways Rangers could not have chosen a more controversial character to break their

The Big Man and the Quiet Man reunited at Parkhead.

tradition of sectarianism, and time alone will tell if Maurice Johnston can handle it all.

One thing I can say is if Rangers had come in for me when I was a player I would have signed for them if the money had been good enough. Naturally, as a professional I would have tried for them as much as anybody else. People may find that hard to believe, but it is true. Maybe Maurice Johnston's only mistake was to go on about how much he loved Celtic. Fair enough, maybe he did, but he is a professional like the rest of us and it is a bit of kidology to pretend to the fans that there is anything more important than what cash is on the table and what are the terms in your contract. At the end of the day that pays your rent, not how much you love Celtic, Rangers . . . or Arbroath for that matter.

Most of all it would be interesting to hear Bill McMurdo's version of what went on throughout the whole affair. I am sure he could get quite a few bob if he ever sells that story. He grew up a couple of hundred yards down the road from me in Craigmillar and he wasn't a bad wee player if I remember rightly. He was on Hibs' books for a while, but never quite made the grade. Most of all I remember he was a right wee moaner and hated losing. Obviously that will to win has served him well in his last few years as an agent.

I played park football with him as well and the funny thing about those days is religion never came up at all. I still remember the first time hearing someone referred to as a 'bluenose'. There was this big lad who worked in the pits and he had split his nose in an accident. Anyway, the scar across his nose had a blue tinge in it and, innocent young lad that I was, I thought this was the reason people called him a blue nose.

You hear an awful lot about loyalty from managers, directors and the press, but a footballer doesn't owe it to anybody but himself and his family. Celtic, people say, are a bit special in this way, but look at the way even they have treated people who have shown them great loyalty. When you first sign for a club, you're a big cheese as a laddie. Also it may be the team you support, but once you're married with a couple of kids and you've been in the game a bit longer, you realise in many ways it's just a job. It would be nice to think you can be loyal to a club, but unfortunately most players' experiences tell them it doesn't count for much.

However, I believe most players are willing to be loyal to their clubs in the first place, but because of the way clubs treat them they do not deserve loyalty. But you will notice how many really good players take great pride in their job, and you only have to watch them training. At

Doing the double with Celtic. I run off at Hampden a happy man after we had beaten Rangers 1-0 in the cup final in 1977. The week before we had clinched the League title.

Celtic I saw it with the likes of Lennox and McGrain. At Easter Road I would have advised any young lad to train beside the likes of O'Rourke, Blackley or Stewart. Pick up good habits and stay away from the rogues.

The loyalty issue is getting complicated with agents now in the game. I don't like the image it is giving football these days. I don't know Frank McAvennie, but I do know he's a good player. The same can be said for Maurice Johnston. However, the coverage they have received in the papers about their champagne lifestyle does not do professional football any good. It gives ammunition to those who want to criticise footballers and portray them as idiots who don't know what to do with all the money they have. Most footballers don't go to Stringfellows or drink champagne. Nor are they just a bunch of upstarts who can only kick a ball about. My experience is most players are not like that, but that is not good newspaper copy. When Scotland were in Argentina the press latched on to certain players, but there were any number in that party they could have talked to whom they would have got some sense out of. The press don't seem to be interested in normal, well-behaved people.

I do realise that these young players are under different pressures from my day and they get offered money for all sorts of stuff. Also living in Glasgow for guys like Frank McAvennie and Maurice Johnston must have been no easy thing when you're under the spotlight all the time.

These were issues Jock Stein cared about. He didn't expect players to be angels and somehow he knew everything that was going on, but he never let you forget you were representing Celtic. I went on tour with Celtic to Singapore and Australia where we played in a tournament with Red Star Belgrade and Arsenal. Alan Hudson and Malcolm MacDonald got sent home, but somehow nobody would step out of line with Stein. It was on this tour that I had my run-in with Busko Lukic of Red Star. But as I've said, Stein could see my point. There are limits to good behaviour.

It was just at the start of the next season that I picked up the injury that was to finish my playing career. We were playing Dundee United and as I turned to go after a ball with Paul Sturrock something went with my knee. At half-time I was in trouble, as you cannot play at the back carrying an injury as you can up front. I went in for a cartilage operation which usually only takes three days, but I got hepatitis. I lost a couple of stones in weight and was hobbling about on crutches for months. So I missed virtually the whole of that season. It was also a turning point for Celtic as Jock Stein moved on for his brief spell at Leeds and Billy McNeill took over as boss.

I was 34 now, and whereas I had hoped to play till I was 35 or 36, I realised my time was up in a League Cup fixture with Montrose. Wee things were in my game that had not been there before. I was taking that crucial bit longer to turn and the space I operated in became smaller. Maybe I could have got over it, but it's doubtful. One time the ball came to me and instead of turning on it as I would have normally done, I booted it into the stand. That was it. After the game I told Big Billy I was packing it in.

Some players get hurt early in their career, but I had always been very lucky. I had only ever had a couple of broken toes. Of course I was disappointed as I could have picked up a few more medals no doubt at Parkhead, but looking back I had been very lucky and had years of good fun. Celtic also played in my testimonial where 25,000 turned out at Easter Road. I actually enjoyed the game which often is not the case on these occasions. Despite the fact I had been away for over a year, the Hibs fans were great to me and Celtic brought through a support too. Alan Rough had an exceptional game that day which led to his being reselected for Scotland.

Also there was the inevitable penalty that falls to the player whose day it is. I had squared it with Peter Latchford the day before that he would let me score. Sure enough, the Hibs team I was playing in for the occasion got a penalty. Up I stepped, placed the ball and looked up to see there was no Peter Latchford. Roy Baines instead was in goal and I hadn't noticed. I started nodding to Roy, telling him where I was going to put it, but he couldn't hear for the crowd shouting. So I said, 'Forget it', but it was no problem anyway as I sent him the wrong way.

CHAPTER NINE

The Northern Star Rising

IT was a strange feeling I had on the first free Saturday after I left Celtic. Every footballer has to come to terms with it at some time, but there I was staring out the window on a rainy day and my wife turned to me and asked what I was going to do. I thought about it for a minute and told her I really didn't know. Then I thought: there is only one thing for it. I'll go to a game. So I headed for Tynecastle where Hearts were playing Aberdeen.

Outside the ground I got approached by an Aberdeen fan who asked me if I would like a ticket. I accepted it from the guy but little did I know then he was to become a good friend of mine. Anyway I went up into the stand and as I took my seat an old man said, 'Do you know who used to sit there?' Not surprisingly I didn't and he told me it was Willie Bauld's seat. 'Well,' I told him, 'that'll do me nicely, pal.' Aberdeen won that day and within two weeks I was their assistant manager. Also by the end of the following season I was to win the league with them at, of all places, Easter Road. It was also to be my last game with the club and also Hibs' last game in the Premier League for over a season as they were relegated. Meanwhile I was to have my first taste of the management business and spend just under two very enjoyable seasons with Aberdeen.

I had always thought I would like to try management and had started going on coaching courses to Largs in my early 20s. It served two purposes as it kept you fit for two weeks during the close season and you could see if you could pick anything up about the game. It was there that I first got to know Alex Ferguson. I knew him already as a player and had always found him an annoying bugger to play against. But at Largs we got to know each other better and always got on well. We shared a lot of views on the game and were to have a good friendship when we worked together at Aberdeen.

The two weeks at Largs were good fun and you learned a lot as well. You also got some crackers coming along for the course. There is one I remember but I won't name him as it would be cruel to his family. We had just watched a video of Johann Cruyff and were to discuss aspects of his play and his tactical awareness. Well, this fellow was asked to lead off. What did he think of Cruyff? 'He's a bit greedy.' I couldn't believe it, but it was to get worse. Anything else about him? 'Aye, his left foot's no as good as his right.' By now the lecturer was giving up, but he thought he'd give the guy one last chance. 'Anything more you could say about Johann Cruyff?' 'He doesnae speak very good English.'

That was an extreme case, but if people ever say Scottish football is parochial, you can understand them if they've come across the likes of that character. At that time Bobby Clark, Gordon Wallace and Archie Knox were regulars and among the coaches were Eddie Turnbull, Willie Ormond and Jimmy Bonthrone and John Haggart. A lot of people went down there to pick brains and were not saying too much themselves. Eddie Turnbull was very good in that situation and so was Jimmy Bonthrone. We also got foreign guests but a lot of it was too technical. I think there is a happy blend between the boot-up-the-park brigade and those who want to get out the blueprints. It wasn't all work, and in the dining room it got a bit like a school camp at times. You all had to take turns at washing dishes and big John Hughes of the Celtic tried to skive off his turn. So the wee wifie started shouting at him to get into the kitchen. The whole place erupted like Alcatraz with everyone banging the tables chanting 'Yogi'. He was marched away to roll his sleeves up. Another time Eusebio was a guest and on the final night a bit too much was had to drink and here was Eusebio looking a bit baffled at the top table with John Haggart serenading him with 'I'll Tak the High Road' and 'Stop Yer Tickling Jock'.

Anyway, I immediately accepted Alex's offer to join him in Aberdeen. Big Billy McNeill had just left, missing out on the league by one point the season before. However, it wasn't all plain sailing for Alex and he had to win a lot of people over to start with. Some of the older players had played against him and that would not endear anyone to Alex. Also he had just been involved with a tribunal when he left St Mirren and his argument with their chairman Yuill Craig. The first thing he set out to do was get his own team. You could tell something was going to happen because there were good players coming through. McLeish and Strachan were in the reserves and Simpson, Black and Cooper were appearing on the scene. Jim Leighton was just starting out and Mark McGhee arrived from Newcastle. Joe Harper had also returned and no one can argue with his record second time around.

Stevie Archibald had been brought from Clyde by Billy McNeill. We felt he was playing too far out and encouraged him to get right into the box where he could be most effective. Stevie, though, was the sort who would give you a good game even if you played him at full back. He wasn't your run-of-the-mill guy and was very single-minded. We used to travel down and stay in the Excelsior at Glasgow Airport if we were playing Rangers. This freezing cold Saturday morning I sent the players out for a walk to stretch their legs and loosen up a bit. I watched them all come down and go out through the foyer. Archibald arrives and steps outside, looks both ways, shudders, about turns and comes back in. I stopped him: 'You're supposed to go for a walk.' 'I did,' he says. 'You never. I saw you. All you did was walk outside the door.' I then told him I would have to report it to Alex if he didn't do it. So off he goes into the lift. Five minutes later he is back down the stairs wearing slacks and just a tee shirt. He looked at me as if to say, 'I'm away for a walk', and off he went striding out into the sub-zero temperature. You could say Stevie had his own way of doing things. But he was never any trouble at training and that is one of the key areas in which I judge a player. You do the business there and you won't have much to worry about elsewhere. Willie Miller was a good enough trainer when we took over but his attitude was a bit casual. He just came in to pass the day on Monday and Tuesday. I told him that people looked to him as captain and followed his example. Also when he was 28 or 29, time would have taken its toll and you just cannot become a good player then. I think he listened and Willie has gone on to have a tremendous career and he is a great support to other players on the field.

They were a good bunch of lads and we knew we had a team here if we got a bit of luck and handled them just right. One of the early lads I felt sorry for was Stewart Kennedy who teamed up with big Rougvie at full back. Stewart got his bad injury and was to miss out on a few medals he would otherwise have collected. He also had a great burst of pace but we told him he started his run too early in his own half so the opposition could see him coming. We got him to hold back until he was about thirty yards out and then let fly and he proved very effective at it.

Fergie is a tremendous enthusiast who lives for the game. He set a high standard at Aberdeen and he made sure it didn't drop. He had a thorough knowledge and really went at things. Players can weigh you up in about ten minutes and tell if you know what you're talking about.

It was a nice break watching a reserve game as there was never the same pressure as is evident from this picture when I was at Aberdeen. Brian Scott, now Celtic's physio, was then at Aberdeen.

He quickly won the players' respect and he could also mix well with them and pick the right time to do it. If Alex had a fault it was that he was too honest with people, particularly the press. They should have known at times when he didn't mean to be quoted.

Also around this time, Jock Stein gave me a bit of advice that it would not be a bad idea if we got a reputation for being a real hard lot. Then you start getting your results at Ibrox and Parkhead and people will start to sit up and take notice of you.

Another great point with Fergie was what he considered the most important relationship in football for a manager. It was not with your players or the press or the fans. It was your relationship with your chairman, and at Aberdeen he was very lucky to have a first-class one. Dick Donald was a terrific chairman. At even the wee clubs board meetings are a regular event but Fergie was never bothered with them at Aberdeen. Dick Donald let him get on with managing the football side of things. Fergie would bump into Dick in the corridor and they would stop and discuss something there and then. At other clubs you can get called to meetings all the time and you end up talking round in circles.

Dick was also someone you could trust, along with Chris Anderson who was a very good administrator, and had very good ideas about the future of the game. Travelling on the bus I would often end up in long conversations with both of them. The key to success at Aberdeen was harmony. Also we used to pick up Dick at his house when we were going away and he would always come on with bags of sweeties he would pass round. We even had a regular driver called George. When George wasn't there it was a case of 'Where's George?' and the inference was: who's this other guy?

In our first season we got to the League Cup final after beating Hibs in the semi-final. Although we lost to Rangers, we learned a lesson that day. We were one up through Duncan Davidson but when the equaliser went in three Aberdeen players went down on their knees. Now that was a sign they were beaten and they would have been as well waving their wee white flags. I turned to Alex and said we would be as well taking off these three now. We spoke to them later and explained how terrible their attitude was and I'm glad to say these guys never repeated it and went on to beat Rangers regularly. It was also a big let down not getting to open the champagne on the way back up, but as I told Alex McLeish: remember this feeling when the good times come and you will have learned a lot. Also don't worry because there will be good times. Another thing you soon learn in football is you learn more from defeats than you do from victories.

Fergie and I would also go off after a game for a few pints and run over what went wrong and what went right. He could talk football all night. There is a lot to him as a character and he could be great fun with his little quirks. He was also one for coming out with the strangest of things. A couple of Fergieisms were: 'Have you ever seen a Pakistani funeral?' or 'Have you ever seen an Italian with a cold?' He would just come out with them and that would be it. You would be left to ponder what he meant.

Another major achievement of Fergie's was tying up local youth with the club. Whenever someone ended up down south as Denis Law had, at least the club knew about him first. A fine crop of local lads came through in Hewitt, Simpson, Black and Cooper.

It was also a change for me being in management where you had to start being aware of how everyone was feeling. Before as a player you didn't even put away your own boots after a game. All you cared about was your personal performance and that was it. Now you were bothered about every knock a player took. On Mondays with some players you knew there was no way they would be fit for Saturday whereas there were others like Willie Miller who could be very doubtful on a Thursday but by Saturday he would be playing. The worst thing, though, as a manager is watching: you are about to shout 'Don't do that!' and then you think, 'Why can they not see that for themselves?'

In our first season we also reached the semi-finals of the cup, but were beaten 2-1. I had no qualms or special feeling about playing Hibs. All I wanted was a result, but it was Hibs who got it. However, I was really rooting for them when they played Rangers in the final which they lost in the second replay. We also had a couple of good older pros in Drew Jarvie and Bobby Clark, who were a good influence on the team. Both were fitness fanatics and Bobby was different from a lot of goalkeepers as he would express his opinions and get involved in overall tactics. Most goalkeepers I have found tend just to sit in the corner and not join in. You also find some players have nothing to say, ever. Then there are the other ones who never shut up. Stewart Kennedy was the barrack room lawyer at Pittodrie. At the end of a tactics talk Fergie would know it was coming. Stewart would always pull him up to explain something in greater detail. Although these sorts of players can be a real pain, you really like it as it shows some spirit.

Also at that time I began applying aspects of man management that I had picked up over the years. You cannot treat every player the same. You can give a good player a hard time as he will go out of his way to prove you wrong and he has the confidence to know he can do it. You can shout and bawl all you like at other players who have limited talent but it won't make them any better. Also when you want to make a general point, you pick on one of the top players who has stepped out of line, not one of the reserves.

We were also in the European Cup Winners' Cup that season and Bobby Clark and I went on a spying mission to Marek in Bulgaria. When we came back we were careful about what we told the players. You don't want to build the opposition up too much because it might be 80 minutes into the game before your own team really starts playing and finds out what they're really like. When I was a player I would never watch the opposition warming up as, if it is a big name club and they are doing fancy work with the ball, you can easily begin to overrate them.

In Bulgaria Bobby and I were given an interpreter with a Hollywood accent. He went everywhere with us and he took us to meet their officials in the hotel we would be staying in. They asked what food the players would like and started to run through a day's menu. We told them our breakfast would be tea, toast, bacon, eggs. Our Hollywood friend disappeared and came back with a plate of bacon and eggs. So Bobby and I had to taste it. Then we got on to lunch. We had hardly mentioned the word steak and he was away again. Five minutes later he was back with two steaks on a plate. Once more Bobby and I had to taste it. Everything we mentioned foodwise they brought out from the kitchen for us to eat and we were full up for the next two days.

While we were there I asked Bobby what he fancied doing on the Sunday. He said, 'Did I not tell you I had to go back to Glasgow to see a specialist?' No way was I staying in Bulgaria on my own! If I had, I reckon I would never have been seen again. So I flew back to Glasgow with Bobby, met the Aberdeen party and virtually flew back out to Bulgaria again.

We were knocked out in the next round by Fortuna Düsseldorf of West Germany. Although we won 2-0 at Pittodrie, we had made unbelievable mistakes over there to lose 3-0. You soon learn how some players get frightened on the big occasion and make mistakes, whereas a good player will nearly always do the right thing at the right time. Also, you have to point out to Scots players that if you lift your boot it's a foul in Europe. You see it all the time in Scotland, so when they get penalised over there they get rattled and feel that the foreign referee is biased against them. Another problem for Scottish players abroad is how they drop off you and let you play. Scottish teams can often fall into the trap of slowing down not just physically, but mentally as well, and lose their concentration. You are often at your most vulnerable around their box when you lose the ball. Next thing you know five of them are bursting out of their half and battering down on your goal. In the Premier League you never get to go ten yards unchallenged, but when you see a player left on the ball you can really tell his worth.

At Aberdeen we tried to make the players aware of what was happening around them, and cut out the aimless high balls into the penalty box. We adapted our system to our players but made sure they played the ball to each other's feet. I know that sounds obvious but it is surprising how many footballers cannot get it into their heads to do just that. By the beginning of our second season we felt we were getting it right and reached the League Cup final which we lost 2-0 to Dundee United in the replay after the original 0-0 draw. It was another disappointment but United were a good team and you knew they were going to go on to better things. However, on our way to the final we had beaten Rangers and Celtic. That season we went on to play Rangers seven times and they beat us only once; we played Celtic six times and they too beat us only once. It had now begun to dawn on the players they were going to go all the way.

Also in Aberdeen they had the advantage of being up there on their own and the local press concentrated on just them. It gives them that bit of confidence and the whole city backs the team. Despite everything going so well I had decided to leave Aberdeen and try management on my own. I made my announcement at the New Year and Alex was the first to know of my decision. A lot of people still ask me why I did it, but I just wanted to try it on my own. Fergie recognised my reasons and I would have regretted it if I had never tried it. Many would have been happy in my position and I didn't have an alternative fixed up. I told Fergie I would leave at the end of the season.

It turned out I left in the best possible way as we won the league. Ironically it was at Easter Road again. I was sad to see Hibs slipping and also what made up the Hibs team that day. Unfortunately there was hardly any quality in it. It was a summer's day when we came to Easter Road and I remember coming along London Road and the Aberdeen fans were sitting under the trees. It looked like a red army waiting to march. I know the Aberdeen support is often criticised and it can be very quiet at times, but that day we took a great support. Behind our dug-out there was someone with a transistor and Roland Arnott, our physio, kept asking how Celtic were doing at Love Street. I didn't want to hear and told Roland to tell the guy to get away from us. We won 5-0 and at the whistle we had to look up to the Aberdeen journalists in the press box for a signal to see if we had won.

We had done it, although at one stage we had been ten points behind Celtic. Then our run had started. Often when it happens you aren't aware of it at first, as the first two or three results are scrambled. Looking back I could see it was a home game at Pittodrie against Morton. There had been a blizzard and we worked to clear the pitch.

You wondered at the time if it was worth it especially if we lost. But we scraped home 1-0. Three of our last four games were away from home which was a tall order for any side. When we drew 1-1 at Tannadice we felt we had done it, although it was the first goal we had let in for 16 hours of play.

I felt Fergie and I had covered a lot of ground in a short spell. It was Aberdeen's first title in twenty-five years and Fergie was the toast of the town. I had plenty of time since the New Year to change my mind but decided against it. Looking back, it hadn't all been easy for Fergie. A lot of people looked on him as this young upstart challenging the Old Firm but he knew how important it was to break them down before you can win anything in Scotland.

Fergie went on to great achievements with Aberdeen and I will always remember the night they won the European Cup Winners' Cup against Real Madrid. Aberdeen were a great club to work for and the people were special. Teddy Scott, the trainer, was a smashing guy. He had played in the last Aberdeen team to win the league and did a hundred and one jobs for the club. He also kept a tight grip on his store room as players will lift anything given half the chance, and if you got an invite into it from Teddy it was a privilege. You had been invited into the inner sanctum.

The man behind it all — Dick Donald — was down there every day and you would always know he was there as you would hear him whistling. Although Dick owned a lot of businesses, he was a very plain man and never hit you over the head with who he was. However, as far as the club went it was his ball and you had better not forget it. The only time I was ever worried about falling out with him was when Fergie and I went to Copenhagen. We got the kick-off time wrong and while we were supposed to be at the game we were watching naughty films. It was only when we came out and got a taxi to take us to the game we were told it was over. Alastair Guthrie from the *Press & Journal* had come over with us and he was saying to me, 'What am I going to tell my editor?' I told him in no uncertain terms I couldn't care less what he told his editor; it was Dick Donald I was worried about. Fergie and I realised we had no option but to come clean with Dick. All he said was: 'Were the films any good?'

Dick never interfered, but he was on the ball. One thing he was particularly keen on was he liked the pitch to be in good condition. It was his baby and you would often see him walking about the park with the old groundsman. The relationship between board and management was quite the opposite from what lay ahead for me at Easter Road and it only reinforced Fergie's view about the relationship between manager and chairman being all-important.

CHAPTER TEN

Going It Alone in the Kingdom

ALTHOUGH Alex Ferguson had asked me to reconsider staying on as his assistant, I was definite about going it alone. One of my first offers was from a mining company in Zambia who asked me to manage their side but my wife came out with the classic 'You can go on your own'. So that was that settled; I returned to Edinburgh and just before the start of the 1980/81 season I got a call from Cowdenbeath.

Their chairman was Charles Gronbach, but it was a director Eric Mitchell who called me. I was keen to take the job as it didn't matter whether I was with a top club or not. I wanted to build my own team and be my own boss. In time I might move on but I wasn't thinking too far ahead. I wanted to test myself and I liked Cowdenbeath's approach. You often find the people who run wee clubs are great enthusiasts and are more genuine about their involvement in football than others. Obviously, with bigger clubs the power and the status are great attractions for people. But if you're involved with a club like Cowdenbeath, these are hardly likely to be your reward.

It was a different world from Aberdeen altogether. Although some of what I might have said about Aberdeen may give the impression it was a homely club, it was also run in an extremely professional and successful manner. Dick Donald and company were not flash, but they knew they were a big club and made sure everyone else knew they were one of the biggest clubs in Scotland.

But at Cowdenbeath I soon realised there was a difference. One night at training in my first week the floodlights suddenly went off. The players didn't seem to be phased by this and just kept on training. I asked what the score was and was nonchalantly told, 'That will be the chairman. He comes and puts the lights out to save money.' I had to go in and ask for them to be put back on. From then on we trained under the floodlights.

On a Thursday night after training I would put the team list up and one night a player tapped me on the back. 'I cannae make it on Saturday. It's my sister's wedding.' The big question now was: what were we going to do for a player? However, we did have good players there. Andy Rolland who had been with Dundee United was the captain and once again he was a really good pro, full of enthusiasm and a good example for other players. Billy Steel who had been with Rangers was there and also Grant Tierney who is now with Dunfermline. I also spotted Norrie McCathie playing at the Jack Kane Centre in Craigmillar and invited him over to Cowdenbeath the next evening. Norrie was to move on to Dunfermline when I went there and is still doing a good job for them.

Although I was only there for less than six months, we got a few good results. One game in particular I remember was against Clyde. They were playing well and were top of the second division. So I got Willie Murray, the former Hibs player, to turn out for us. Willie was heading off to Australia, but he played that night and had a stormer. We won 4-2 and after the match the chairman came up to me. 'Where did you get that laddie?' I told him he was only here on loan and we couldn't sign him as he was going to Australia. 'Oh no,' he said. 'He can't go to Australia. He'll sign for us.' But I did explain to the chairman that Willie did not play like that in every game, so Cowdenbeath freed Willie to go down under.

There was another time when the huge gap between the top tier and the bottom division was really brought home to me. During a game a fight started on the terracing, but it must have been between two pals as that sort of thing was unheard of at Cowdenbeath. Meanwhile, one of our players had got injured and I turned to our physio Jimmy Reekie on the bench, but he wasn't there. I asked the substitute where he was and he pointed up to the terracing. There was Jimmy tending to one of the guys in the fight who had a bleeding nose, while our player was lying injured on the park. As you can gather, it was a rather carefree attitude.

But it was a very good club with a smashing support who had an excellent social club. I used to get a laugh every Monday morning when the old groundsman would be out on the pitch cursing and swearing. They had stock car racing on a Sunday and sometimes the cars would cut across the pitch leaving skid marks and lumps of rusty exhaust pipes. Another time in a reserve game the referee got hammered in the face with the ball. We carried him into the dressing room concussed and got a doctor. He had driven over from Edinburgh, but as the doctor examined him he said the ref was in no fit state to drive back. All you could hear was the groundsman growling in the background, 'I'd let him bloody well drive!'

I may have had a shortage of players when I went to Easter Road, but at Cowdenbeath it was something else altogether. One game we called in a 'ringer' and gave him somebody else's name. However, what does the 'ringer' do but go and get sent off? So when the 'real' player turned up the next night I had to tell him, 'You're not playing on Saturday.' He looked a bit nonplussed and asked why. I explained: 'You were sent off last night.' It took a minute to sink in with him while I gave him a fuller explanation of what had happened. He was not the best-behaved of players either, but he was forever complaining about this slur on his disciplinary record. There was also the rule you could only have three trialists in a game but I have always thought this was ridiculous as smaller clubs often do not have enough players.

Throughout my time at Cowdenbeath, I had George Stewart as my assistant. He was my very first signing and I had to go over to see Cecil Graham, the Hibs secretary, to be shown how to fill in the forms properly. George was to come with me to Dunfermline and Hibs. He had a terrific attitude and was a bonus wherever he went. Not long after he arrived he was sent off and the next day I got a call from Stewart Brown of the *Evening News*. Stewart asked me, 'What's the Big Yin been up to?' and I said, 'You know what he's like but he'll only miss one game.' But obviously Stewart knew something we did not. Big George had amassed quite a few penalty points at Easter Road and brought them with him to Fife. It is often tough luck on a club when they inherit a player's disciplinary record along with his services.

I felt we were going somewhere at Cowdenbeath, but after less than six months Dunfermline approached me to join them when Harry Melrose left. So in the New Year of 1981 I moved across Fife to Dunfermline. I am pleased to see Dunfermline doing well these last few seasons and they are obviously now a forward-looking club, but when I first went there all you got out of the board was the early '60s. They were a very good side then, but you have to move with the times and not live in the past.

One of the first things I did when I moved there was ban the players from using the Paragon Club behind the stand. The players would go down to Dunfermline's social club after the game and a lot of people were not too pleased about this. I had nothing against the Paragon Club, but I didn't think players should mix with fans immediately after a game. That is when you get all the back-stabbing with players forming into cliques. They can blame each other and be indiscreet about their team mates.

Dunfermline have refulfilled their potential as a big club, but when I was there they too had their wee touches just like Cowdenbeath. We were training on a frosty night and Sandy McNaughton arrived, but he was without Mick Leonard who usually travelled through from the west with him. So I asked where he was. Sandy mumbled, 'Mick'll no be here tonight,' and went in to get changed. I called over to the trainer Joe Nelson, 'Where is Mick?' Same answer: 'Mick'll no be here tonight,' and Joe continued getting all the gear ready. Later on I took Joe aside and said, 'Everybody here seems to know why Mick'll no be here tonight bar for me. Would you mind letting me in on it?' He looked at me as if I was a bit stupid. 'You've seen the roads tonight?'

'Aye.'

'It's awfie icy.'

'Aye.'

'So he'll no be here tonight.'

'There, you've gone and said it again,' I groaned. 'But why will he no be here?'

'He'll be driving the gritting lorry.'

So any time after that while George and I were driving over from Edinburgh and there was a touch of frost, he would turn to me and say, 'Aye, Mick'll no be here tonight.'

There was a more serious side to life at Dunfermline and I came across one of the worst incidents in my career when Jim Brown got his leg broken by John Pelosi of St Johnstone. I had brought Jim over at the start of my second season and although 'Bomber' was not our best player he was our most influential. He was a good trainer, had plenty of experience and was very good on the pitch with young players. Such a player is a great asset to a club as he can bring on players better than a manager will. He is out there on the pitch to correct their mistakes while they make them so they pick up good habits right away. It is like everything: 'on the job' training is better than any amount of theory or practice.

But when we lost Jim we never got over it for the rest of that season. There was no doubt that Pelosi played him. It was a grim tackle and Pelosi got a lot of stick for it and received a long suspension. But his career kept going while that was the end of Jim's. I know football is a hard game and a contact sport but there is no place for that sort of thing. Going over the ball at a man is the worst thing you can do in the game.

You also often find that it is the more skilful players who do it as well. It is not so bad dealing with your 'hammer throwers' as you can usually see them coming a mile away and that's what you expect from these big, rough types. But when someone goes over the ball it is often as a player is making a clearance or playing a through ball. Everyone follows the ball as the culprit puts his boot in. The referee then turns to see this crumpled heap. It is a nasty thing that I always felt was unnecessary. The recent most controversial case of this kind was Neil Simspon's foul on Ian Durrant at Pittodrie. It was a great shame for Durrant, but I would have said Neil Simpson would have been the last person to do that deliberately. I was one of his bosses at Aberdeen and he was a very nice lad and a hard, but fair, player.

Although every club has its ruffians, at Dunfermline I had quite a well-educated team. Our keeper, big Hughie Whyte, was a doctor, as was our right back Bobby Robertson. The left back, Bonar Mercer, was an accountant and qualified pilot. They were nice guys and great enthusiasts, but sometimes I thought they had wasted their youth reading too many books instead of kicking a ball about. Sandy McNaughton, one of our forwards, was a teacher and his job and the board's penny pinching could have cost us relegation. We were playing Motherwell near the end of the season and it was a very important game to keep us clear of the relegation zone. It was the most important ninety minutes of the whole season. Anyway Sandy told me after the Saturday game he would not be able to make it on Wednesday night against Motherwell as he would be taking a party of schoolkids to Aviemore. He didn't have a car so he couldn't make it down. I spelled out to him in no uncertain terms that this ninety minutes was the most important of our season. He had to play so he must hire a car to get down to East End in time. Sandy hired the car and scored the winner as we beat Motherwell 2-1, but I couldn't believe it when I was hauled up at the next board meeting for extravagant expenses. What was this, I was asked, about players hiring cars? Sandy had scored the winner that kept them clear of relegation and someone was quibbling about the cost of hiring a car. I did not mince my words and let them know my feelings. I also asked them to consider the cost of hiring a bus through to Stranraer next season if they had been relegated.

While I was at Dunfermline I was also quite optimistic about our progress and knew they had the biggest potential of the smaller clubs in Scotland. Jim Leishman started helping out with the reserves when I was there. He was not speaking to God in those days, but you could spot straight away his love for the club. It was a pleasure working with guys like him and George Stewart. You know where you are with someone like George as he is what you see. There are no dark corners. George also had a lot of good ideas about the game. I remember one game he suggested that when the opposition got a corner we should leave three players up the park instead of one or two. Anyway, you ought to have seen the stushie the other team got into. George's thinking was: if your goalkeeper is good at handling crosses and you have a centre half who is good in the air, you can easily handle two or three forwards. When you do something out of the ordinary you can really throw people. Also if you adopt an attacking approach it is interesting how you really frighten teams.

We had a lot of work to do at Dunfermline, but we went into the close season confident we could be contenders in the next season. The club had fallen into the habit of not looking too far ahead, but we felt we could change that. Once that happened, Dunfermline would have a lot of potential once more. Jim Leishman has gone on to prove that, but before we could go any further with them, I got the call from the one club I could never turn down. I never hesitated for a minute about taking the Hibs job and knew there were so many people who wanted me to take it. But I knew there would be a lot of problems and could feel already things were not quite right at the club.

CHAPTER ELEVEN

The People's Choice

When I got the chance to return to Hibs it came right out of the blue, but I must admit in my heart I had always hoped to go back to Hibs. However, being in the game so long your head often tells you it is a mistake to go back again and I always had that in the back of my mind while I was Hibs manager.

At that time, though, I had my hands full at Dunfermline and didn't think my chance of the Hibs job would come up for some years. I had no idea Bertie Auld was going to get the sack. You don't like to see anyone lose their job, but that is part of football life. As a player you compete for a place in the team and are used to ousting guys. Likewise, you know that someone is always gunning for your position.

But it meant a lot to me returning to Easter Road and I got a great reception from Hibs fans in Edinburgh. I always felt the fans wanted me more than the board. That is probably why the board went for me as I was the people's choice. I knew standards had fallen dramatically at Easter Road, but I was not quite prepared for how far standards had dropped. One thing I wanted to make sure was that I had people I could trust as my assistants. I couldn't have made a better choice than Jimmy O'Rourke and George Stewart.

We got off to a really poor start and soon found ourselves at the bottom of the Premier League along with Motherwell. The biggest threat you can have over a player is to leave him out, but I never felt I had that option at Easter Road. Money was limited and although I signed Mike Conroy from Celtic and Willie Irvine from Motherwell, I had to draft in Malcolm Robertson, the former Hearts player, after a chance meeting with him at Waverley station. We had limited resources but we had to beat Motherwell in our first meeting with them. We were sweating a bit before that game and a few people at the club questioned signing Malcolm short-term, but he played well and Gordon Rae got our winner to let us breathe a little more easily.

Troubles were mounting up and we soon lost goalkeeper Jim McArthur. But we then made what I think was a great move for Hibs. I had had Alan Rough in mind all along and contacted Peter Cormack who was boss at Partick Thistle. Peter was not happy to let him go, but it was a wonder he hadn't been signed before. An awful lot of that was to do with the English press. Just before we got him I was watching the BBC's Saturday lunchtime show and they showed the top five keepers in England. Then they switched to Scotland with a clip of Roughie making a mistake. I noticed they never showed Ray Clemence letting the ball through his legs at Hampden often, but they prejudiced the whole case against Roughie. However, if it helped us to get him more easily, I was thankful for that.

I had total faith in Alan and knew he would prove me right. He was very laid back and had no nerves. Maybe that misled people, but Rough wanted to win as much as anyone. You get players who rant, rave and shake their fists, but often it is just an image. The quiet man wants to win just as much as anyone else.

With Jimmy and George, I went out of my way to create a good atmosphere at Easter Road as the last thing we wanted was it to be like a dentist's waiting room. We had a running joke that Jimmy was Roughie's batman. The team would be just about to go out when Roughie would say, 'Jimmy, have you seen my gloves?' That would get Jimmy going, scurrying around searching for them. The players would join in the patter, asking, 'James, are you sure Alan has his hat?'

Having Roughie come at that time was good for the club as it gave us a bit of standing. He intimidated opposition forwards and had a good dressing-room manner. He was good with young players and he was the sort of guy who would talk to the Prime Minister in exactly the same way he would talk to the youngest ball boy at Easter Road. The only thing I did not like about Roughie was his habit of going on mazy dribbles. I would look the other way and say to George Stewart, 'Tell me when he's finished.' He also had another habit of turning round and asking the ball boys what time it was. I often think he was more interested if they were off in the 3.40 at Kempton Park than how long it was to half-time.

Alan, like most goalkeepers I have known, was a good trainer and was marvellous in his first game where we got a draw at Morton followed by another against Rangers. Then Gary Murray got our winner in another

victory against Motherwell. By now we had plenty of enthusiasm in the
team, but I knew we did not have the talent to go any further. The
players we had would just keep us where we were. It was difficult to give
some of them a hard time as they would just go on making the same
mistakes till they retired. I didn't want to shatter the confidence of
people who didn't have much of it in the first place. During my playing
career and at Aberdeen I felt free to give people a piece of my mind, but
in management with Cowdenbeath, Dunfermline and Hibs I always had
to bite my tongue.

In training at Aberdeen you could tell Strachan to start hitting balls
thirty yards across the park to someone. At Easter Road in my playing
days Alex Edwards and Cropley could do that spot-on ninety-nine
times out of a hundred. However, there were some players at Hibs who
could keep you waiting all day before they got on target just once.

But things had improved and we then went a three-month spell when
only Celtic and Aberdeen beat us. Confidence spread from Roughie
through the team. We also had Gordon Rae and Jackie McNamara, two
players who gave their all for Hibs.

Alongside there was Alan Sneddon who has had his critics, but he
always gave 100 per cent. Alan also had a dip in his career, but he
bounced back from that which is a sure sign of character.

Just about every Saturday till the end of that season I thought about
relegation and at the same time I was worrying about what lay ahead in
the next season. The fundamental problems at the club were not going
to go away and we badly needed new players. Just at the end of the
season we got a real confidence booster when we beat Kilmarnock 8-1
even though we had to play Graham Harvey who had come from junior
side Ormiston Primose straight into the first team. That was an
indication of the extent to which standards had dropped. You could
never have done that ten years earlier as the gap would have been too
great.

I found forward planning a big problem, but George and Jimmy
mucked in with me. Every day before training the three of us would
have a cup of tea and think up something to vary it. We would play a
form of baseball where Jimmy would change the rules every day. He had
a good sense of fun and was also excellent at coaching youngsters. The
pair of them really helped keep the players' peckers up. The three of us
would pick the team, but of course I had the final say. We were not
always in agreement but that was the way I wanted it. They were the
type of guys I could turn to and ask to nip down to Newcastle to look at
a player — not that we would get the chance to back it up with any

The People's Choice: Back at Easter Road as manager in 1982.

money — and off they would go straight away. They weren't bothered about time off and were only interested in seeing the club improving all the time. You couldn't put a value on them.

We also tried a few tactical variations and started playing with only three defenders at the back. The first time against Dundee United it took them a while to figure out what we were doing and we got a 3-3 draw, our first result at Tannadice for a long time. We did the same against Aberdeen and told Brian Rice to hit any free kick on the left side of the box around the outside of the wall. Leighton would be at the other end guarding his goal, expecting someone like Ralph Callachan to hit a right footer on the inside of the wall. It worked with Rice scoring and we tried to get our players regularly to do the opposite of what the other team expected.

Despite any progress we were making I was feeling continually frustrated and didn't think the board had the same will to put Hibs back on top as I had. There were many aspects of the way things were run that I did not agree with. Then things came to a head just before we played Motherwell at the end of the 1982/83 season and I told chairman Kenny Waugh I was resigning.

At the end of each season players get freed. When this happens you don't notify them by mail. Instead. you get them into your office and tell them you're sorry, but you're not going to renew their contract. You're letting the player go and you wish him all the best of luck and if there's anything you can do for him, you'll do it.

But here was a case at Easter Road where a young player just got a note out the blue telling him he was freed. The first I knew of it was when he came to me with the letter in his hand. I was really angry it had been done in this way. You only sent someone a letter if you were retaining them and offering them terms for the next season. To be freed is a hell of a disappointment and everyone would like to be told to their face. I was denied this opportunity and had to apologise to him. I would like to think I was man enough to tell someone to his face. It was something that should never have happened. Maybe the club didn't attach much importance to it, but I did. If you have to deal with players, these things are important and I didn't want other players to think the same could happen to them.

I got hold of Kenny Waugh and told him I was not going to Motherwell and that was it. Jimmy and George took the team to Motherwell and Stewart Brown, who knew something was up, carried the story that night in the *Evening News*. Meanwhile I was taking in a game at Craigmillar Crossroads and, if I remember correctly, it wasn't a bad one at that.

Of course there was a big reaction to this with all sorts of people contacting me. On Sunday Kenny Waugh phoned me up at home and asked me to reconsider. Many people think I should never have gone back. The original incident was a silly thing that should never have happened, but, as I said, it was important to me. Lots of things were annoying me about the club. One of them was the amount of trouble players were having with contracts. As far as anything involving the players was concerned, I felt the board should have come to us but they bypassed us nearly always. We also had the dilemma of where our sympathies lay as we had been players ourselves. We understood what they wanted yet at the same time we had to serve the board. When a manager is in his office talking to a player about money he will tell him he is referring it to the board. However, so often he really knows the board will not accept it.

Anyway, I spoke to my father about my resignation and listened to his advice. I decided to reconsider, but with hindsight maybe it was the wrong decision. The same reason that overruled my thoughts when I took the job made me stay on. My heart was with Hibs and I wanted to revive them as a club. I was sorry to see Jimmy and George leave soon after. They had their own reasons, but I believe they were frustrated at the way things were going. We all felt our efforts to get things moving at Easter Road again were going nowhere. Kenny Waugh gave me assurances for me to continue in the job, but I still had no illusions as to how hard the job was going to be. However, I felt I should not walk out on the club and gave the board another chance.

I needed a new assistant and called upon another old team mate. John Blackley who was now at Hamilton asked me to consider him. I made my decision and asked John through as I had known him as a player and had always got on well with him. It shows how things had still not improved when John had to turn out as a player just after he joined us. John himself was to be forced into the same situation with Tommy Craig when he took over. On the Thursday before we played Dundee United we were sitting in the boot room wondering what to do as we had been hit by injuries. Then I looked up at him and said, 'You'll have to do.' He was a bit taken aback and although he had put on a few pounds he was still a class player and proved to be one of the best we had. It was around that time we beat Aberdeen 2-1. They had just won the Cup Winners' Cup so we were pleased to have drawn level with minutes to go. Tom McNiven was sitting beside me and was shouting at a player taking a shy to fling it anywhere, as long as it was up the park. So he heaved a massive shy into their box and Willie Irvine nipped in to get his second and the winner. We were absolutely delighted and couldn't believe we had got a win. I still wonder how we won games when I look back on some of the teams we put out.

I remember another game against Motherwell and we were drawing with a couple of minutes to go. Tom McNiven suggested a substitution to waste a bit of time. I wasn't sure and was wondering who to take off when I heard this fan screaming at me from behind the dug out: 'Stanton, get that bastard Duncan off!'

I thought, 'Right enough, I'll take Arthur off.'

I put on John McGachie who immediately went on a couple of runs, hit the bar and hit a cross over in the last seconds for Brian Rice to make it 2-1. After the game a couple of reporters started going on about my substitution. I even thought they were going to use the word 'inspired'. So I thought I had better come clean and told them, 'That boy should have been sitting in my place on the bench.' Mind you, we never told Arthur about it.

One good thing that was happening was good young players were beginning to emerge for the first time in quite a while. It was unfair on them to expect them to keep the club going in the hurly-burly of the

Premier League, but it was one area where we succeeded in turning the club round. Brian Rice was a great passer and had some left foot. He was also surprisingly good in the air, but I always felt he didn't have enough dig. I tried to tell him you have to let your opposite number know you're there early on in a game and stamp your authority on it with a couple of good tackles. There was no point in waiting till the 70th minute to do it.

Paul Kane was also emerging at this time. There has never been any question about Paul's commitment, but he has still not found his best position. I think it's right back: he can tackle, run and is good in the air. Also he is better facing the play. He is not a forward although he does a job there as he does in midfield. He may be helping the club but he isn't helping himself. If Paul played Hearts every week I'm sure he would be a great player.

Kevin McKee was another who showed some promise, but I think his confidence was ruined a lot by the incident when he was attacked by a fan at Ibrox. I always thought it was strange how that hero went for the youngest guy on the park and I never saw any of them try that on with Erich Schaedler at Ibrox. Michael Weir was another signing, although a lot of people at the time said he was too small. I've always thought that was a load of rubbish. By that mark you wouldn't sign Maradona, Jimmy Johnstone or Billy Bremner. I think Michael could still do more to force himself into the game. When he gets behind a player he tends to chip balls in instead of firing them in low. However, he's a great favourite with the fans and I think there must be something in the air up in Clermiston as it seems to produce real Hibbies.

Other good players coming through were Gordon Hunter and Calum Milne, both tenacious young defenders, and Gordon in particular has a good future in front of him. Another lad we introduced was John Collins. No one can dispute his ability but he cannot go on having people saying he's a great player; he has to go out and prove it. One way would be to score a lot more goals. Many players don't realise you have to make runs from midfield to get into scoring positions. Nine times out of ten you might not get the ball, but that tenth time you have your chance and it's in the back of the net.

At the start of my second season we had the first Edinburgh derby for four seasons due to both Hibs and Hearts being alternatively relegated. We went ahead through Ralph Callachan but they equalised. Then John Robertson was gifted a scoring chance from Ally Brazil for his second. It was a shame for 'Benny' as he had been having a very good game till then. Often he was criticised unfairly. When people said he should never be in the team I would ask who would they have in instead. I never got a satisfactory answer. Benny did a job for us at a time when we were very short of players.

Willie Irvine began to knock in the goals and was ably assisted by Bobby Thompson, public enemy number one. Bobby had skill, but unfortunately his reputation went before him. Sometimes referees were looking out for him, but often you couldn't blame the referee. One time we were sending someone off to see a specialist and someone chipped in that we should be sending Bobby to a psychiatrist. Some of his challenges at times would make you flinch even when you were sitting in the dug-out. It was funny when you spoke to him afterwards. He was like a choirboy. 'Who me, boss? Couldnae be me you're talking about. It must be someone else.' When he lost the head against St Johnstone and pushed the linesman, the needle went to red.

What many people forget about Bobby Thompson was how much he helped Willie Irvine. Willie had a great run for a season and got Hibs' first hat-trick for seven years which once again shows how things had slipped. When Bobby got a six-month suspension we couldn't afford to lose a player for that length of time. The players' union refused to represent him at the SFA. I thought it was a bit unfair as you would have thought he was Jack the Ripper, but they acted as though they were Pontius Pilate and washed their hands of him.

Willie's form began to dip. It was no accident that with big Bobby rampaging down the line keeping defenders busy, Willie picked up a lot of loose balls. You often see that dip when a striker's partner goes. It happened with Willie Pettigrew and Bobby Graham at Motherwell and to Steve Cowan when Gordon Durie left Hibs. Also wee Robbo missed Sandy Clarke when he returned to Hearts. When one goes the other misses the freedom the other created for him.

We went on to finish seventh for the second season running, but the sorest point was our defeat in the cup to East Fife. We drew at home and let down the big support who followed us to Bayview. Early on a couple of free headers were hit straight into the keeper's hands. When I saw that I just knew it was going to be one of those nights. After that result I wanted to have a clear out at Easter Road, but we couldn't afford it. We hadn't enough back-up in playing staff and no money for new players.

Feeling very frustrated, I went into the close season. Arthur Duncan moved on from Hibs to Meadowbank and it was the end of an era. At that point we tried to get Tommy McQueen from Clyde, but Aberdeen snapped him up as Doug Rougvie moved to Chelsea. We also failed in a bid to get Jamie Doyle from Partick. I had also made several inquiries to Jimmy Bonthrone about Gordon Durie after the East Fife game, but the money wasn't there at the time.

I went into the new season not feeling any more optimistic. It started with defeats from Hearts and Meadowbank. In the next game I was sent from the dug-out at Pittodrie by Brian McGinlay for arguing with the linesman. Things were getting worse and when we went to Ibrox Kevin McKee was attacked on the pitch. Overall we still had the same problems and resignation was now on my mind. When Meadowbank beat us in the League Cup people were shouting that we should have beaten them every night of the week. But technically we weren't much better: fitter, yes, but we needed better players.

The Dumbarton game almost seemed like a relegation decider and it was only September. We lost 3-2 and I phoned Kenny Waugh on the Sunday to resign officially. Maybe he and the board felt we were not getting the best out of the players, but no matter who they appointed, they wouldn't have done better with the players there at the time. I think I was proved right and only some buys and the young players coming through have helped since then.

John Blackley's reaction was I should leave it a while and not be rash. But I was not being rash. I just felt I had come to the end of the line with the present regime. John was in a quandary over what he should do but I told him to look after himself. I went back in on the Monday to say cheerio to the players and it was a bitter disappointment to once again be leaving Easter Road on a sour note. You also learn a bit at times like that. I was touched by one or two people's reaction; then again, there were a couple of people I thought I was reasonably close to whose attitude let me down.

I also thought I had always been fair with the press, but I was disappointed by some reports, particularly when Jim Kean reported Kenny Waugh's statement in the *Daily Record* that all communication had broken down between me and the players. As I have said, it made me really angry. In that one sentence he passed judgement on my management. I felt it was irresponsible and he should have balanced it with my own comments rather than just speaking to Kenny Waugh. Similarly, I would not have minded if it had come from someone who was an expert on the game and really had his finger on what was happening at the club.

Any breakdown in communication at Easter Road was not my problem and as long as Kenny Waugh was chairman I felt there would never be the money that was needed to help Hibs turn the corner.

The way I left Easter Road, both as a player and a manager, taught me a few things about life. One of them was not always to believe what people say to your face; rather, you should wait until they back up their words with action.

Despite all that happened, though, it has not affected the way I feel about Hibs and their supporters.

CHAPTER TWELVE

On the Outside Looking In

SINCE I resigned from Hibs I have severed all my links with the game except as a spectator. I am still a regular at Easter Road, but you would never get me back on the bench under present circumstances. The reason is quite simple — I am banned. The SFA imposed this ban on me, like Graeme Souness and quite a few others. The only difference is that while Graeme Souness and others went ahead and served their sentence I did not and have no intention of doing so in the near future. I was also fined £500 at the same time, but that remains unpaid as well.

I was hardly a hooligan as a player, and as a manager I didn't rant and rave in the press or leap about on the track. My crime was that I questioned authority and that was breaking the golden rule as far as the SFA are concerned. I must admit I have never respected authority for its own sake. It has to be earned or worthy of respect. I've never had much time either for the pompous attitude so many people adopt once they get in a position of authority.

I have never set out to be a rebel, but there are times when I said what I thought and didn't just let things pass. I never felt I lost the head and went about it in my own manner, but maybe in some ways that makes it even worse for those you're confronting. I also know people might say I have a chip on my shoulder, but they can think that if they like. I feel I never got a fair deal from the SFA and neither did Hibs. And while they continue to operate as they do, they deserve the criticism they get. I know many people in the game who agree with me, but will not talk out for various reasons.

As a player I was sent off three times. Once against St Johnstone and another time against Red Star Belgrade. Both times I foolishly retaliated. Maybe when the Yugoslav hit me I should have collapsed in a heap and rolled about on the ground for a while so he would get sent off. But I never thought that way and instead lost my temper and hit him back. My other sending off was with Hibs against Dunfermline. Alan Evans, who later joined Aston Villa, went for a ball with me near the corner flag. We fell over together as the ball went out and both got up to go back in for a corner. Meanwhile the linesman was waving his flag and the referee called me over. He told me I was being sent off as the linesman saw me hit Evans. I was taken aback and Alan Evans looked baffled as well. I hadn't touched him but that was it. However, when I went up before the SFA there was a letter there from Alan Evans saying I had never touched him, so I got off.

One thing I would like to see introduced into football is the rugby rule where you are penalised a further ten metres if you do not move back in time or argue with the ref. If this was brought into football it would wipe out so many forms of cheating at one stroke. Dissent would vanish overnight. Players would know if they talked out of turn they could put their team in a very dangerous position. The reaction of their own team, the manager and fans to them giving away a goal because of their big mouth would soon curb such behaviour.

However, as a manager you are in a different position. My first run-in with officials when I was in management came when I was at Aberdeen. I was fined £25 by the SFA for comments to the referee after a game at Ibrox. During the game he just awarded Rangers their decisions but when Aberdeen got a foul he would start to do a mime. I asked him why he was doing that and I could tell he didn't like the question or what I was inferring. He said he was doing it to explain to the crowd why he had made the decision. I thought I had made my point but he reported me to the SFA for being out of turn and I got my fine.

Whenever I approached a referee after a game I would deliberately try and be calm and civil with him. If the referee hasn't had a good game he can be in a bit of a state. He knows he has had a bad game and the crowd has let him know it and very often it is they who are not in control. Anyway my first major fall-out with an official was at Easter Road after a Celtic game with Bobby Valentine.

When I was up before the disciplinary committee they kept bringing up the word 'agitated'. I asked why they were bringing up this word when I had not been agitated. I didn't swear at Bobby Valentine. I had civilly asked him a question he couldn't answer. Valentine had booked Willie Irvine as he was finishing off a move. He whistled but Willie followed through and put the ball in the net. It is very difficult to expect a player to pull up spot-on every time, especially when he's in a goal-scoring position. Then later on in the game a Celtic player deliberately booted the ball away at a corner but it bounced off the terracing fence and came back onto the pitch.

After the game I asked Valentine why he had booked Willie Irvine for kicking the ball away and not the Celtic player. He replied that the Celtic player was trying to kick the ball over to the corner flag for Arthur Duncan to take it. Well, any professional knows that you just don't do that. But I didn't want the Celtic player booked. I was just wanting the referee to be fair. He then asked me to leave his room, telling me I was booked and he was reporting me to the SFA. At the meeting he said it was the first time he had ever to ask a manager to leave his room.

The SFA asked me if I had anything to say and I replied, 'What's the point? You're only going to listen to him.' I was fined £200 but that was not the end of the story. It was not posted by Hibs in time and my fine was doubled. I ended up having to pay the extra £200 myself because of a clerical error on Hibs' part in not posting the first cheque on time. Ernie Walker made a comment in the press at the time that I was being 'indiscreet'. This further annoyed me as here was Ernie Walker able to chip in when I couldn't say anything as it would prejudice my case. He wasn't even on the disciplinary committee.

I felt hard done by and was not looking forward to any further appearance before them as I was sure I would not get a fair deal. Then a couple of weeks before I resigned we were at Pittodrie when the linesman flagged Graham Harvey for being offside. Later that night on television it was evident he was not offside but at the time I said something to the linesman. Often they just leave it or tell you to behave. This time the linesman called over referee Brian McGinlay and he sent me to the stand. I felt the linesman knew he was wrong, but he had to back himself up and McGinlay had to take the linesman's point of view. When I came through to Park Gardens they obviously thought they should double my fine from the last time and, in the event of my taking up any post in football, I was banned from the touchline for one year. At the same time the hooligan who had run on to the pitch at Ibrox and assaulted Kevin McKee was fined only £100 in the courts.

I feel there are a lot of double standards in football, especially the higher up you go. Unfair pressures are put on managers and people like Ernie Walker have said it is up to the clubs as they are the SFA. But it is these same clubs that have created the system that makes managers lose the rag. It is all very well for directors to lose the head or SFA people to say things in the heat of the moment, but not for a manager. These same people will give him the sack if doesn't get results. So while his livelihood is being threatened he is just supposed to sit there. Football is a passionate game and people get over-involved. Managers are going to make mistakes, shout and bawl and get out of order. I am not saying it is right but the same people who punish him are the ones that create the system.

The pressures are incredible and it is difficult to think of a manager who has not been in trouble at sometime. Jim McLean hit it on the nail when he said that the nastiness in football had even crept into the directors' box. So what chance have you got at the sharp end of the stick down in the dug-out? I don't regret the way I behaved as a manager and would not go back in time to make sure I didn't ruffle anybody's feathers. What I did was not out of order. If I really believed I was in the wrong it would be a different matter.

As I said, the pressure on managers nowadays is incredible, but I also have my doubts about the high profile managers have. If you ask anyone about the Famous Five they can name the players, but I bet a lot of people don't know who the manager was. However, we have seen the cult of the manager develop over the years and recently it has got out of hand. So much media attention revolves around them, and now what actually happens on the park is almost secondary. I do not think it is good for football, but probably an even more worrying trend is the new media stars — the chairmen and managing directors. In some cases they are the main focus of press attention. Surely Scottish football is not in such a bad state that players are of little interest so we have to focus on those who run the clubs and make the deals. It is a thing football people should bear in mind and make sure they do not lose sight of their priorities. The fans are the lifeblood of the game, not sponsors who come and go, and what the fans are interested in is the players and how they perform on the park.

One part of my football career I do have regrets about is my international career. When I was with Celtic I was called up by Willie Ormond to go as an over-age player along with Bobby Clark with the under-21s to Pilsen in Czechoslovakia. Jock Stein told me Willie had been on to him about it. My first reaction was that I didn't want to go. Stein immediately said, 'I know why you don't want to go.'

'Why is that then?' I replied.

'They never picked you for Scotland when you were younger and instead chose players who were nowhere near as good as you. I understand how you feel, but go anyway. It won't do you any harm and you can help younger players through their first international experience.'

Once again Jock Stein was right. I was annoyed how I had been passed over throughout the years. I don't care what anybody says but if I had played for another club, particularly Rangers, it would have been a different matter. A lot of mediocre players got Scotland caps because as they wore one blue jersey people thought they could fit easily into another. I am glad to say it has changed to a considerable degree but they still have an undue influence. I also know that Willie Miller felt the same way for a long time. You get fed up making up the numbers when you know you should be playing but because you are not with the right club and certain people in the press are not touting for you they pass you over. Willie was left out in the cold for a long time after making a fine debut against Rumania. It was only when he won the league with Aberdeen that the Glasgow press sat up and took notice. Only then was he reconsidered.

I played sixteen full internationals for Scotland and must have sat out the same number again on the bench. My first honour was when I was called in to the Scottish League team to play England at St James's Park, Newcastle in March 1966, after Bobby Murdoch was injured. I played at the back and although England had Jimmy Greaves, Jack and Bobby Charlton and Alan Ball playing for them, we won 3-1. Not long after that I was capped at under-23 level and again we beat England who once more turned out a first-rate team with Colin Bell, Peter Osgood, Martin Chivers, Brian Kidd and Rodney Marsh in their forward line. I never played against England in a full international, but had the chance in 1973 at Wembley. I had captained the side against Wales and Northern Ireland in the Home Internationals and could have gone on to Wembley. I felt obliged to pull out of the team as I was carrying an injury and it wouldn't have been fair on the rest of the lads, but I was sorely tempted.

My first full cap came against Holland just before the World Cup in 1966 and I played alongside Ronnie McKinnon of Rangers at the back. It was an 'all tartan' team which was not too fashionable in those days, but they were trying it out after we had failed to qualify for the World Cup. Holland were described as a 'third rate' football nation by some of the Scottish press. Well, this 'third rate' team went on to whip us 3-0 and their best player that night was left winger Piet Kaiser. He would do a wee shuffle at the halfway line and in the next stride he would be at the eighteen-yard line. He was hitting them in from 40 yards that night and there was not a lot we could do. However, I was proud to get my first cap. It was what every player dreams about. In some ways it doesn't matter at that time if you don't get another as you have got there in the first place. It is the pinnacle of your career. After the Holland game there was a reaction against many of that team and I didn't get another cap till 1969.

That was in a 1-1 draw at Hampden against Northern Ireland. George Best was playing that night and proved to me he was one of the greatest footballers ever. I always thought it was a touch of class that Hibs brought him to Easter Road and it was typical of Tom Hart's big thinking. I got another couple of caps that season against Eire and Austria and one against Denmark the following season. The next year 1971 I was capped seven times when Tommy Docherty was boss and with his typically understated manner he told the press, 'Pat Stanton is better than Bobby Moore.' Under Docherty I pulled out of Scotland's tour to Brazil because my wife was ill. It was a genuine call-off and I had a doctor's line, but the 'Doc' banned Charlie Cooke and myself and said we would never be picked again. However, he was a big enough man not to stick rigidly to that and he recalled me.

The Doc parted ways with Scotland to join Manchester United and Willie Ormond took over. I only got another four caps — two against Wales, one versus Northern Ireland and my final one in West Germany. Willie Ormond was underestimated as a manager and he was a fine judge of a player. An achievement of his that is played down is St Johnstone's European experience; I don't think there are many who could have done that. My last international was in West Germany in the warm-up to the World Cup in 1974 where I was joined by team mate Erich Schaedler. However, I never got to go to the World Cup there and it was a disappointment.

I had been to Germany before with Scotland, but was on the bench when Tommy Gemmell got sent off in the 1970 World Cup qualifier. Big Tam had chased Helmut Haller halfway across the pitch in the opposite direction from the ball and booted him up the backside. Not surprisingly he was sent off and as he made his way to the dressing room I was told to go with him to keep him company as he was getting a hostile reception from the Germans. The crowd were throwing everything bar the kitchen sink at him as he neared the tunnel. So I told the bench they must be joking. If they were that bothered about keeping Tam company they could go themselves.

Another eventful foreign trip was when we went on the summer tour in 1971 with Bobby Brown. That team was a real ragbag of nomads. There were so many call-offs I think they took whoever was hanging around the doors as we left. There was Davie Robb from Aberdeen, Bobby Watson of Motherwell and Hugh Curran and Frank Munro from Wolves to name a few. I captained the side in Moscow and we played well although we lost 1-0. I always remember meeting big Al Shesternev, the Russian captain, at a reception after the game. He was an excellent player and had played in Rest of the World selects and here he was letting everyone in Moscow know he had travelled. While the rest were togged out in demob suits big Al had on this amazing Rupert the Bear jacket that would have made even Arthur Montford jealous. It was yellow with big red and brown checks. Of course, over there it was a great status symbol, but as one of our lads said he probably got it in the Barras and Coco the Clown had the trousers.

That was also the season I scored my one and only goal for Scotland. We were playing Portugal and I sliced a beautiful banana shot into my own goal which left Bobby Clark with no chance. As Bobby picked the ball out of the net he shouted over at me, 'Hey, Stanton, how come you always manage to score against me?' That was just after the occasion where I had broken his shut-out record for Aberdeen a few weeks earlier at Easter Road. I was substituted that night in Lisbon and wasn't too pleased about it. I could see someone getting the hook and looked behind me to see who it was, but there was no one there. Apart from the goal I had been playing well, but that is just part of the game you have to accept.

That season we also played Belgium twice in the European Nations' Cup. We were hammered 3-0 on the famous mud heap at Liége which I described as reminding me of Pumpherston with its huge bing at one end of the ground. In the replay Kenny Dalglish made his debut for Scotland coming on for Alex Cropley as a substitute, and John O'Hare of Derby County got our winner. Also I had the pleasure of meeting Johann Cruyff and Johan Neeskens that season after we were beaten 2-1 in Holland.

In both international and European football I came up against some great players. There was Puskas with Real Madrid and Altafini, once with Napoli and the other time with Juventus. Other Juventus players who impressed me were Franco Causio and Fabio Capello. Then there were players like big Al Shesternev and the great Germans, Beckenbauer and Breitner. I have mentioned Cruyff and Neeskens, but another Dutch player who really impressed was Wim van Hannegan, the man who tore Celtic apart in the European Cup Final for Feyenoord. But I must say the player who impressed me the most was George Best, undoubtedly the greatest that I actually played against. He would even have given Willie Hamilton a run for his money.

Now I watch most of my football at Easter Road and the players I particularly like in Scotland in recent seasons are Paul McStay, Ray Wilkins and Jim Bett. Also Ian Durrant has shown great promise and has that great ability for a midfield man of getting into the box and scoring. His injury was a blow to the Scottish game and hopefully it will not have a long-term effect on his future. Of course as a Hibs fan I would say John Collins has great ability. I had watched him a couple of times when I was Hibs manager and could tell he was special, and of course signed him. However, he still has to properly fulfill his promise and could take a leaf out of Durrant's book and get into the box for scoring positions. I hope by now this advice is not necessary for John and he stays at Hibs, but he will be a hard one to hold onto.

It is very satisfying when you are a manager to see young players come through and start to fulfill the promise you thought they had. Despite my problems at Easter Road I think I left them with a fine crop of emerging talent. Hibs have always had one or two good players coming through the ranks apart from a fall-off in the late '70s. However, I hope such a fall-off doesn't reoccur as unfortunately there don't seem to be too many around at the moment. A club like Hibs will never be able to compete with the big clubs on the transfer market and has to produce its own talent. Dundee United are one club that have shown everyone up in that department in recent years.

I have mentioned already my belief that many boys are bypassed because players are creamed off at too early an age. But young boys must continue to master the basic skills of passing and receiving the ball. These are the two things that happen most in a game. If you're able to control the ball with one touch, you give yourself two or three yards immediately. If it takes two or three touches, an opponent will be on top of you before you know it. These skills are picked up with hours of practice as a boy on the streets and in the back greens. A player should have these basics when he arrives at a club. He can still afford to be a bit raw, but you can work on that. But time and again I will tell a lad to make sure his passing is perfect. It is more important than dribbling or any other part of the game. In the Hibs team that won the League Cup everyone could pass the ball bar Arthur Duncan and Erich Schaedler, but they had their own special attributes.

In recent years Liverpool are the best example of a passing team and the European teams can show us a thing or two. I welcome the spread of satellite television if it makes this point. Also a really good pass gives the receiver time to control it just using one touch. When I went into the game I felt I had these basics mastered, but I still practised on it. Another great skill that should be emphasised is timing your runs perfectly so you arrive in the right place at the right time. A lot of great players are prepared to make that twenty-yard run and not get the ball, but too often you just see players who only like to play when the ball is at their feet. Steve Archibald's arrival at Hibs provided the young lads like Collins and others with a great example of what a player should be like. He has a tremendous first touch and is aware of space. That is half the key to success as a manager — making players aware of space. Even when the goalkeeper had the ball in his box Archibald would be moving around looking for a position to take up. Archibald plays when the ball is fifty yards away while some players only do it when it's five yards away.

Jock Stein was the first to drum into me awareness of space and how to use it when the ball is on the other side of the field. Eddie Turnbull was also strong in this department, and so often at Hibs you would see this working so simply with Alex Cropley hitting a crossfield ball to Alex Edwards. Jimmy O'Rourke would have been in between them, but he would move ten yards forward at exactly the right time, taking a marker with him. A path would now be clear for Cropley to make his move. A slower-thinking player wouldn't have noticed this, but Jimmy's ten-yard run would have opened up the field. Cropley would fire over the perfect pass and Mickey would receive it perfectly on his toe. Simple stuff, but Eddie Turnbull knew he needed smart players to do it and it was the basis of some great football at Easter Road.

Now I've been away from the game for too long I don't want to get back into it. I am quite happy to sit in the stand watching Hibs and wait for the good times to roll again at Easter Road. However, one thing is for sure: now that I sit in the stand, I am a better player than I ever was.

Index